WILD HORSES AND THEIR MANAGEMENT BY THE BUREAU OF LAND MANAGEMENT

WILD HORSES AND THEIR MANAGEMENT BY THE BUREAU OF LAND MANAGEMENT

MATHEW O. ARDUS
EDITOR

Nova Science Publishers, Inc.
New York

LIBRARY OF CONGRESS CATALOGING-IN-PUBLICATION DATA
Available upon request

ISBN 978-1-60692-9

Published by Nova Science Publishers, Inc.; New York

CONTENTS

PREFACE

Following passage of the Wild Free-Roaming Horses and Burros Act in 1971, limits for the number of horses on each herd unit (referred to as Herd Management Areas or HMA's) were set. These limits or population goals are referred to as Appropriate Management Levels or AMLs. From 1980 and through the present, more active management reduced wild horse numbers closer to AMLs. Wild horse numbers were reduced to about 40,000 by 1999 and to about 37,186 wild horses in 2003, prior to the foaling season. Some 203 HMAs are managed by the BLM across the Western U.S. The responsibility of monitoring range conditions; allocating range resources between horses, livestock, and wildlife; monitoring horse and burro numbers and managing their population levels represents a large federal management responsibility. The number of animals in most herds are counted or estimated every three to four years, in order to plan for any gathers, and adoptions. Herd management activities, such as gathers and removals, take place for most herd areas every four years.

Chapter 1 - The Wild Free-Roaming Horses and Burros Act of 1971 (Public Law 92-195) provided protection for all wild horses and burros on federal lands and provided guidance for their management as a wildland species. At the time the Act was passed, a roughly estimated 17,000 wild horses occupied federal lands designated for the protection. Since 1971, the primary responsibility for management of the wild equids on federal lands has fallen primarily to the Bureau of Land Management (BLM), with the U.S. Forest Service sharing some responsibility. In 1971, the BLM was neither staffed nor prepared to monitor and manage such a large number of horses and their effects on semiarid ecosystems. By 1980, the number of wild horses had increased to 65,000-80,000 animals.

Following passage of the Act in 1971, limits for the number of horses on each herd unit (referred to as Herd Management Areas or HMA's) were set. These limits or population goals are referred to as Appropriate Management Levels or AMLs. From 1980 and through the present, more active management reduced wild horse numbers closer to AMLs. Wild horse numbers were reduced to about 40,000 by 1999 and to about 37,186 wild horses in 2003, prior to the foaling season. This number still substantially exceeds limits recommended by the BLM. Aggressive efforts are planned to reduce numbers to the established AMLs during the next few years.

Some 203 HMAs are managed by the BLM across the Western U.S. The responsibility of monitoring range conditions; allocating range resources between horses, livestock, and wildlife; monitoring horse and burro numbers and managing their population levels represents a large federal management responsibility. The number of animals in most herds are counted or estimated every three to four years, in order to plan for any gathers, and adoptions. Herd management activities, such as gathers and removals, take place for most herd areas every four years.

Chapter 2 - An aerial survey technique combining simultaneous double-count and sightability bias correction methodologies was used to estimate the population of wild horses inhabiting Adobe Town and Salt Wells Creek Herd Management Areas, Wyoming. Based on 5 surveys over 4 years, we conclude that the technique produced estimates consistent with the known number of horses removed between surveys and an annual population growth rate of 16.2 percent per year. Therefore, evidence from this series of surveys supports the validity of this survey method. Our results also indicate that the ability of aerial observers to see horse groups is very strongly dependent on skill of the individual observer, size of the horse group, and vegetation cover. It is also more modestly dependent on the ruggedness of the terrain and the position of the sun relative to the observer. We further conclude that censuses, or uncorrected raw counts, are inadequate estimates of population size for this herd. Such uncorrected counts were all undercounts in our trials, and varied in magnitude from year to year and observer to observer. As of April 2007, we estimate that the population of the Adobe Town /Salt Wells Creek complex is 906 horses with a 95 percent confidence interval ranging from 857 to 981 horses.

Chapter 3 - BLM has made significant progress in setting and meeting AML for the HMAs. As of February 2008, BLM has set AML for 197 out of 199 HMAs. Most of the field offices we surveyed considered similar factors in determining AML, such as rangeland conditions and climate data; however, BLM has not provided specific formal guidance to the field offices on how to set AML. BLM has been working on revising the program's handbook to provide this guidance since 2006. Without clear guidance, BLM cannot ensure that the factors considered in future AML revisions will be consistent across HMAs, especially since the personnel most familiar with the current, informal practice of determining AML are retiring at an increasing rate. At the national level, BLM was closer to meeting AML in 2007 than in any other year since AMLs were first reported in 1984. Specifically, in February 2007, BLM estimated the population of wild horses and burros to be 28,563, about 1,000 animals over AML. To reach this level, BLM has reduced the nationwide population in the wild by about 40 percent since 2000. Our 1990 report was critical of BLM's decisions on the number of wild horses and burros to remove from the range. At that time we concluded that the decisions were made without adequate information about range carrying capacity or the impact of the animals on range conditions. Since then, in August 2005, BLM updated its formal policy on gathers and removals and specified the key factors that should be considered in the decision making process. The extent to which BLM has actually met AML depends on the accuracy of its population counts. Nineteen of the 26 field officials we surveyed used the direct-count method for their most recent gathers. This method, according to researchers, consistently undercounts animals and does not provide a statistical range of population estimates. Some BLM officials are concerned that other counting methods would require too much additional staff or are too expensive. However, undercounting is also costly since it often leads BLM to remove fewer animals than needed, which leads to overpopulation and costlier gathers in the future. For example, in the summer of 2007, BLM staff on an HMA in Nevada miscalculated the population by approximately 640 wild horses and found that the actual population was about five times greater than what they determined was sustainable. Many of the wild horses subsequently removed from this HMA were in poor condition due to severe drought, and about 150 animals ultimately died from disease in short-term holding as a result.

In: Wild Horses and etheir Management ...
Editor: Mathew O. Ardus, pp. 1-36
ISBN 978-1-60692-962-9

Chapter 1

STRATEGIC RESEARCH PLAN WILD HORSE AND BURRO MANAGEMENT: THE BUREAU OF LAND MANAGEMENT, WILD HORSE AND BURRO PROGRAM U.S. DEPARTMENT OF INTERIOR*

U.S. Geological Survey
Biological Resources Division and Animal and Plant Health Inspection Service, Fort Collins, Colorado

I. STATEMENT OF THE CHALLENGE

* This is an edited, excerpted and augmented edition of a Bureau of Land Management, Wild Horse and Burro Program U.S. Department of Interior publication.

A. Introduction Background

The Wild Free-Roaming Horses and Burros Act of 1971 (Public Law 92-195) provided protection for all wild horses and burros on federal lands and provided guidance for their management as a wildland species. At the time the Act was passed, a roughly estimated 17,000 wild horses[1] occupied federal lands designated for the protection. Since 1971, the primary responsibility for management of the wild equids on federal lands has fallen primarily to the Bureau of Land Management (BLM), with the U.S. Forest Service sharing some responsibility. In 1971, the BLM was neither staffed nor prepared to monitor and manage such a large number of horses and their effects on semiarid ecosystems. By 1980, the number of wild horses had increased to 65,000-80,000 animals.

Following passage of the Act in 1971, limits for the number of horses on each herd unit (referred to as Herd Management Areas or HMA's) were set. These limits or population goals are referred to as Appropriate Management Levels or AMLs. From 1980 and through the present, more active management reduced wild horse numbers closer to AMLs. Wild horse numbers were reduced to about 40,000 by 1999 and to about 37,186 wild horses in 2003, prior to the foaling season. This number still substantially exceeds limits recommended by the BLM. Aggressive efforts are planned to reduce numbers to the established AMLs during the next few years.

Some 203 HMAs are managed by the BLM across the Western U.S. The responsibility of monitoring range conditions; allocating range resources between horses, livestock, and wildlife; monitoring horse and burro numbers and managing their population levels represents a large federal management responsibility. The number of animals in most herds are counted or estimated every three to four years, in order to plan for any gathers, and adoptions. Herd management activities, such as gathers and removals, take place for most herd areas every four years.

Mandates

The Wild Free-Roaming Horses and Burros Act of 1971

In this Act, Congress stated that wild free-roaming horses and burros were living symbols of the historic and pioneer spirit of the West; that they contributed to the diversity of life forms within the Nation and enrich the lives of the American people; and that these horses and burros were fast disappearing from the American scene. Congress mandated that wild free-roaming horses and burros be protected from capture, branding, harassment, or death. To accomplish this, these animals were to be considered, on public lands where they were found in 1971, an integral part of the natural system.

Other Statutory Regulations

The Taylor Grazing Act of 1934 authorized the formation of the Grazing Service (subsequently the BLM) and empowered that Service to responsibly manage grazing pressures on federal rangelands. This act accelerated the capture and removal of the wild equids, which were primarily used as pet food at that time.

The 1959 Wild Horse Annie Act (named after Mrs. Velma Johnston) prohibited hunting or harassment of wild horses on public lands using motorized vehicles or aircraft.

The Federal Land Policy and Management Act of 1976 (FLPMA, PL-43, 1701) directed the BLM to scientifically manage rangelands under the principles of use and sustained yield. Under FLPMA, wild horses and burros were one of several multiple uses (along with recreation, mining, domestic grazing, fish and wildlife) that the BLM must manage in combination to best meet the public's present and future needs. Sustainability implies the "maintenance in perpetuity" of yields from public lands.

The Public Rangeland Improvement Act of 1978 (PRIA) amended PL-92-195, and defined excess horses, mandated research and provided guidance for titles for adopted horses and the adoption process.

The Stake Holders

The Bureau of Land Management (BLM)

The BLM's role is to manage wild horse and burro populations on western rangelands for the enjoyment of the American public. In order not to let horse and burro numbers threaten other species, or their own welfare, BLM set animal limits based on habitat and forage, and to monitor effects of various management levels on soil, vegetation, wildlife, and other ecosystem components. Grazing on public domain was primarily unregulated until 1934, at which time the Taylor Grazing Act empowered the BLM to responsibly manage grazing levels on these lands. The BLM's Wild Horse and Burro (WH&B) Program is directed from a central policy office (Washington Office, WO) in Washington, D.C., and an operations office (National Program Office, NPO) in Reno, Nevada. The BLM's 65 full- time equivalent employees, responsible for the management of wild horses and burros are supervised by decentralized operating levels of eleven state offices and several district or field offices in each state, each of which is managed by a state director.

The U.S. Geological Survey, Biological Resources Discipline

The U.S. Geological Survey (USGS) was established by the Organic Act of 1879 to provide geological, topographic and hydrologic information to the nation. This information includes maps, databases, and reports of the analysis and interpretation of water, energy, and mineral resources, land surfaces, geologic structures, natural hazards, and dynamic processes of the earth.

In 1996, the then National Biological Service was incorporated into the USGS as their new "Biological Resources Discipline" with primary goals to (1) assess and report on the nation's biological resources; (2) characterize natural processes and identify factors that influence the nation's biological resources at all levels of biological organization; (3) facilitate sound management with agency partners; (4) provide leadership in developing a biological information infrastructure; and (5) integrate ecological research, inventory and monitoring efforts throughout the USGS.

The USGS-BRD has the capability as the primary research agency within the U.S. Department of Interior not only to gather much of the essential data and to conduct valuable, long-term research for the BLM, but also to engage specialists from other agencies and institutions and to develop interdisciplinary teams to generate the high-quality science needed for informed, science-based management decisions. In late 2000, the primary role for the coordination of USGS-BRD wild horse and burro research was delegated to the Fort Collins Science Center (USGS-BRD) located in Fort Collins, Colorado.

The USDA Animal and Plant Health Inspection Service (APHIS)

Founded in 1862 by President Abraham Lincoln, the United States Department of Agriculture (USDA) mission includes working for a healthy and productive nation in harmony with the land. In this context, the mission of the APHIS includes protecting America's animal resources by monitoring and managing animal disease conditions existing in the United States, resolving trade issues related to animal health, and ensuring the humane care and treatment of animals.

An advisory relationship was created between the BLM and APHIS in February 1999 to allow APHIS to provide assistance, consultation, and coordination on issues relating to the health and proper handling of wild horses and burros that are under the management of the BLM. Through a reimbursable agreement, the APHIS receives needed budgetary support for the wild horse and burro activities of its field force who facilitate the agency's ability to respond to emergency disease outbreaks and provide animal health monitoring and surveillance.

Domestic Livestock Grazers and Wildlife Groups

Domestic cattle, sheep, and goats graze many of the federal lands where wild horses and burros are managed. Livestock grazers often feel that wild horses and burros compete with domestic livestock for range forage. Traditional sportsmen and wildlife agencies may also feel wild equids encroach upon their interests to produce harvestable big game from the same areas. These species likely do compete and conflict with each other in some situations, but the BLM's role is to minimize these conflicts. Wild horses and burros are provided habitat on public lands and it is the challenge to the BLM to obtain the common objective of balance among resource users.

Wild Horse Advocates

Wild horses and burros have a considerable following in the American public who consider the animals to be part of their western heritage and aesthetic enjoyment of the federal lands. A number of advocacy groups maintain that wild horses and burros should receive the first preference in any conflicts with other resource uses on lands where they are protected.

The Strategic Planning Process

In late 2000, the Fort Collins Science Center of the US Geological Survey, Biological Resources Division (USGS-BRD) was charged with developing a strategic research plan for the management of wild horses and burros. Later, contributions by APHIS were incorporated into the research planning process to help address issues related to health and handling. The purpose of this strategic planning process was to:

- review past progress and identify problems;
- set broad goals central to the BLM's mission for wild horse and burro management;
- establish specific, time-bound, measurable goals, and strategies to achieve them; and evaluate the progress towards those goals at set time periods, and to readjust the planning as needed.

Strategic plans are long-range, broad-based documents that create a specifically stated vision of the future. Strategic planning is the long-term directional planning that occurs at the highest level of the program (in this case, wild horse and burro research) and determines the overall success or failure of the program. Strategic plans are one functional segment of a Comprehensive Management System (Organization of Wildlife Planners 1997). First, an inventory and assessment is made of the current state of the research, the client's and stakeholder's needs, and the driving policies and legislative mandates (Figure 1). Second, a strategic plan is developed by the agency in collaboration with the other stakeholders. It details roles, responsibilities, objectives and the tasks that must be accomplished to arrive at the objectives. Third, an operational plan is developed to clarify and quantify the tasks, and outline the process to achieve the objectives. Last, periodic evaluation points are established to monitor the success of attaining clearly stated performance measures and performance standards. The strategic plan is intended to be modified to the extent necessary, at three to five year intervals, based upon these periodic evaluations of progress by the BLM. These steps are repeated until all of the objectives are met, projected in this instance to require one decade.

This strategic plan is a joint effort of the USGS-BRD, the BLM, and the APHIS. This plan was developed to provide the BLM with a research strategy to meet the needs for management and care of wild horses and burros. The plan was developed over a period of 9 months with the input of 39 subject area experts from 11 universities, 3 federal agencies (BLM, USGS-BRD, APHIS), and two state wildlife agencies. USGS-BRD took the lead role in planning and coordinating meetings of the expert committees and in drafting the strategic plan based on committee and agency inputs (compilers, F. Singer and M. Tobler). Assisting in this effort was the BLM's wild horse and burro research coordinator, L. Coates-Markle, and equine health experts from the APHIS, L. Hatcher, and A. Kane.

The strategic research planning incorporated: (1) recommendations from five expert committees in 2001[2], (2) recommendations of the BLM WH&B Advisory Board, (3) direction from the Wild Horse and Burro Act of 1971, (4) input from the BLM managers and specialists assigned to the Wild Horse and Burro Program, (5) periodic milestone decisions by the BLM based upon the research findings and direction, and (6) earlier review of BLM and BRD research (Smith et al. 1996; Gross et al. 1999; Burnham et al. 1999; Population Viability Forum 1999; National Research Council 1991). It was upon this foundation that the strategic plan was built. This strategic plan will be updated at five-year intervals.

There had been no previous prioritization of the BLM's wild horse and burro research and management needs, or no effort to develop a strategy for fulfilling those needs within a specified time period. This strategic planning process will fill this void.

Research Administration and Approvals

The BLM will determine the research priorities for each year with input from the USGS-BRD and the APHIS. A WH&B Research Advisory Committee (also referred to here as the Research Team) will be convened with equal participation by the BLM (the BLM's research coordinator), the USGS-BRD, and the APHIS to provide recommendations to the WH&B Group Manager. A three-member advisory committee is envisioned at this time: F. Singer, L. Coates- Markle, and A. Kane. This committee will meet twice per year to recommend research priorities. One of these meetings will occur in April of each year to coordinate with the BLM's annual budget process. Advice and input will continue to come from the BLM's Advisory Board, the BLM WH&B Group Manager's staff and steering group, BLM Director's Science Advisory Committee, BLM's wild horse and burro specialists, and from any topic-specific advisory panels (seven have been convened to date) that may be convened by USGS-BRD. The Group Manager will meet with the Research Team at least once per year and will resolve any final issues of budgets, priorities, methods, coordination with field specialists, etc. The BLM, as the management agency, must make all final decisions and must set all final research priorities.

Research contracts, cooperative agreements, work orders, and interagency agreements will be administered through the USGS-BRD, Fort Collins Science Center (FORT), APHIS, or the BLM. A logical breakdown of topics will be used according to the appropriate expertise of these agencies on a case-by-case basis. Scientific expertise from the best experts in the scientific community will be sought in any subject area where these agencies and their cooperators can benefit. The APHIS will take the lead role in research dealing with health and handling issues. The USGS-BRD will take the lead role for research as it relates to the assigned topics of contraception, population estimation, genetics and populations modeling.

As the research program grows in funding, the amount of funding to outside experts will likely expand to all subject areas. For those projects conducted by USGS-BRD at FORT, all standard USGS requirements and approvals will be followed including:

1) A written study plan reviewed and approved by two-peer scientists and one statistician.
2) Approval of any animal handlings by the USGS-BRD Animal Care and Use Committee.
3) Center review of all manuscripts and proposals.

USGS-BRD will maintain and manage a core-fund of USGS base research dollars that is earmarked exclusively for wild horse and burro research. Additional USGS funding may come from in-house periodic calls for proposals (USGS Venture Capital Fund, USGS Ecosystems Studies, USGS Species of Federal Concern). USGS scientists submitting proposals will follow the specific proposal guidelines for those programs. The BLM and the USGS may also contribute research dollars in addition to these USGS base dollars.

The competitive call-for-proposals process will be the preferred mechanism for most contracted research, although sole source contracts or university cooperative agreements may be to the advantage of the government in some situations. The Research Team will prepare standard guidelines for the preparation of proposals over the next few months. All proposals assigned to the USGS-BRD for project management must follow USGS contracting requirements that mandate that a panel of qualified specialists rank the proposals. The review panels will include agency representation from BLM, APHIS, and USGS. In addition, more specialized subject experts may be added to these panels.

The Contracting Officer (CO) for the contracts will be the respective agency's regional Contract Officers. The CO Representatives (COR), Project Inspectors, and Technical Advisors will be drawn from the pool of subject area experts from within USGS-BRD, FORT, the APHIS, and the BLM. All these assignments will be determined on a case-by-case basis and may include BLM field resource managers. All unsolicited proposals will also need to follow the same standard guidelines. Some unsolicited proposals may be funded with outside funds, but they still need to fit into the general scope of the BLM's needs, as identified in the planning process, and they should follow the same guidelines for drafting the proposal. Animal Care and Use and other appropriate approval processes must be met exactly as in the case for solicited proposals. Occasionally, exceptional unsolicited proposals will be funded from core research funds. University contractors must obtain the approval of their own university Animal Care and Use Committees before their research proposals may receive final funding approval. For those research organizations with no such approval process, either the APHIS or the USGS-BRD Animal Use and Care Committee will review the handling and care planned, depending upon which agency has been assigned the management of that particular project.

B. Wild Horses in North America

History

The wild horses that roam the west are feral descendents of domestic stock brought to North America by European colonists. No native wild horses existed in the Americas at that time, even though the horse evolved in North America and spread to Eurasia approximately 2.53.0 million years ago. The North American fossil record suggests that progenitors of all extant horses, asses, and zebras once lived in North America.

The last remaining native wild horses persisted in North America until as recently as 8,000-10,000 years ago when they mysteriously became extinct. Recent paleontological finds from Alberta indicate that these last remaining small native wild horses were killed and eaten by Native Americans about 10,000 years ago. Perhaps over-exploitation by Native Americans in this predomestication period played a role in the horse's demise in North America. Climate change and changes in vegetation have likely also played a role (Hulbert 1993, Martin and

Klein 1984, Sharp and Cerling 1998, McFadden 1992). The disappearance of the native form of such an adaptable and widespread species as the wild horse from North America several thousand years ago remains an enigma.

The progenitor of the domestic horse (*Equus caballus*) which was domesticated roughly 6,000 years ago, is suspected to have been a tarpan-like animal—a short, stocky, mousy or yellowish gray (possibly dun or grulla) animal about the size of a large pony. The tarpan persisted into the early to mid 1 800s in western Europe and the Ukraine where the last animal was shot in 1879. The tarpan also did not survive in captivity, the last one died in 1918, although the closely related Mongolian or Przewalski wild horse (*Equus-caballus przewalskii*) did survive in captivity. The Przewalski horse has a different chromosome number and thus, is not the progenitor of the domestic horse (Bennett and Hoffman 1999). Representative examples of tarpan-like animals were reconstructed by breeding the last remaining captive tarpan domestic mixed horses. Tarpan-like animals have recently been released into the wild in several reserves in western Europe. Przewalski horses have also recently been released in the wild into Mongolian reserves.

Horses were reintroduced in North America by the Spaniards during the 1500s. The Spanish or Iberian influence remains very strong in some of the wild horse populations that have the longest histories of escape from domestication (e.g., the Kiger, Pryor Mountain, and Sulphur Mountain herds have strong Spanish ancestries). A number of U.S. western breeds were derived from these earliest Spanish bloodlines (the Spanish Mustang, the Rocky Mountain horse, the Choctaw horse; Bennett 1998). Later however, military, saddle, and draft, stock horses dominated by the Thoroughbred, Morgan, Quarter horse and draft breeds escaped into the western rangelands or were intentionally released and rapidly increased, forming broad zones of introgression with the earlier Iberian Spanish colonial bloodlines. These wild horses of mixed ancestry eventually increased to very large populations that inhabited vast areas of the U.S. western rangelands. Only a small number of the wild horse herds retain a largely Spanish colonial ancestry.

The Management Challenge

Survival rates for wild horses on western public lands are high. None of the significant natural predators from native ranges of the wild horse in Europe and Asia — wolves, brown bears, and possibly one or more of the larger cat species — exist on the wild horse ranges in the western United States (mountain lions and black bears take foals in a few herds, but predation contributes to population limitation in only a handful of herds (e.g., Montgomery Pass). In some cases, adult annual survival rates exceed 95% and many horse herds grow at sustained high rates of 15-22% per year. Prior to herd management, many wild horse ranges were overgrazed, and some wild horses died from malnutrition or dehydration.

Although wild horses occur in 10 states, the vast majority of the animals are located in Nevada (74%) and Wyoming (10%). The BLM has established appropriate management level (AML), or population goals, based on range conditions and monitoring data, while the AML setting process is still underway in other management areas. Current numbers of wild horses are substantially in excess of these goals.

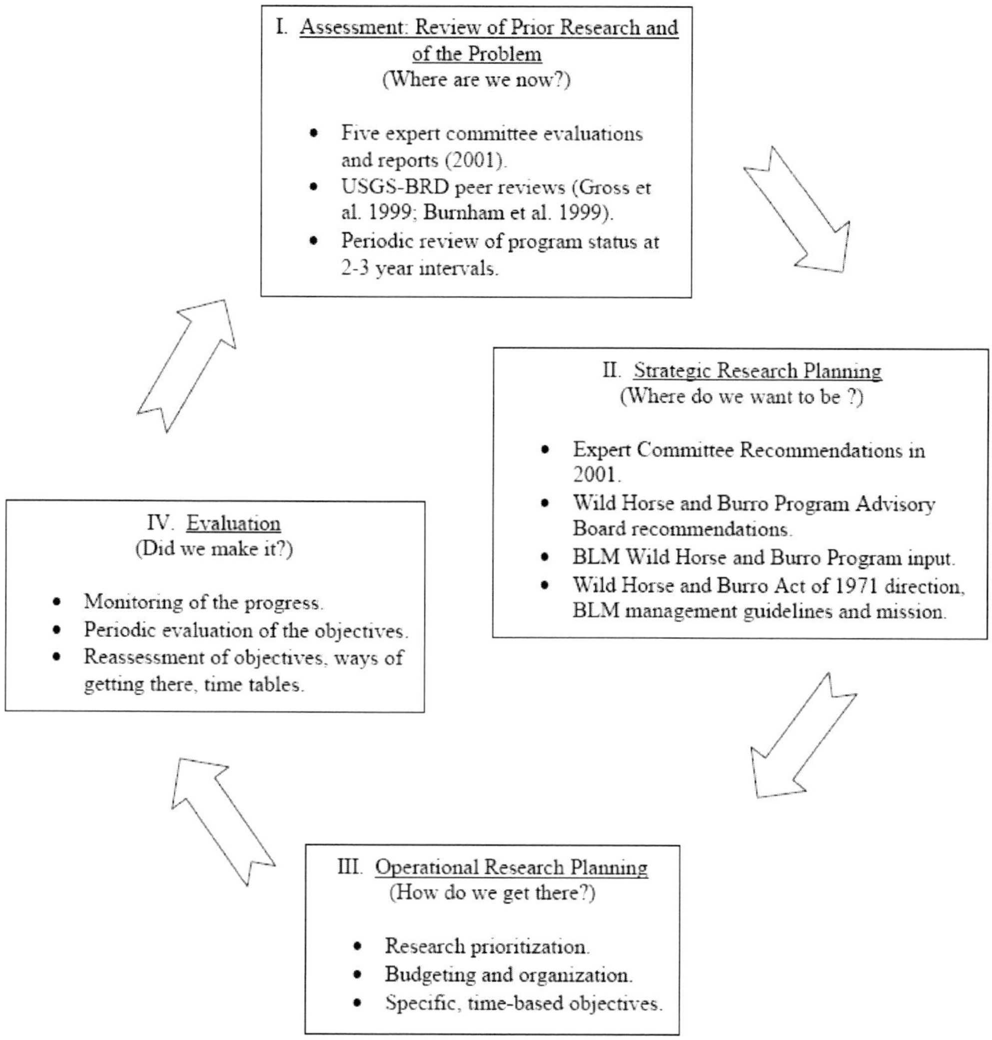

Figure 1. Proposed comprehensive strategic research planning process for wild horse and burro management for the Bureau of Land Management, 2001-2010.

A major challenge for the BLM wild horse managers is what to do with the large number of excess horses produced each year on western rangelands (see Wagner 1983 and National Research Council 1991 for excellent reviews). Once instituted, management in most herds typically involves helicopter gathers and adoption of excess animals. Most horses and burros are adopted by the public, but not all of them can be placed in homes. Older adults, such as some of the mature stallions, are not attractive as potential animals to adopt. Many unadoptable animals are kept for years in captivity in long-term pasture holding facilities. Research into the use of contraceptives to limit the growth of wild horse herds has been ongoing since the 1 970s, both in herds on western rangelands and on several eastern barrier islands. Four of these herds on eastern barrier islands are currently managed with immunocontraceptive agents. Tests with immunocontraceptives have been conducted on a few of the larger wild horse herds in Nevada. However, no free ranging western horse herds have yet been managed at the population level with contraceptives.

Several strong and diverse public interest groups pressure the U.S. Department of the Interior regarding the management of wild horses on public lands. These interests include, at one extreme, those who strongly support the protection and management of wild horses with little or no human intervention. At the other end of the spectrum are those who favor intense management of wild horses and burros, with an objective to maintain very low numbers of horses and burros. Elements of the public, such as those that pursue domestic livestock grazing and the harvest of big game wildlife, may view wild horses and burros as some competitors for other resource uses.

The BLM requires the highest quality science to simultaneously manage for sustainable production of all components of the ecosystem and for healthy, free-roaming, and genetically viable populations of wild horses and burros.

History of Contraceptive Research

The Problem

The BLM's need for a fertility control agent to manage the numbers of wild horses was recognized soon after passage of the Act in 1971. The federal government sought to reduce the number of animals that they needed to gather, transport, adopt, feed and maintain (in the case of non-adoptable animals).

Testosterone Propionate in Stallions

In 1978, the BLM entered into a series of research contracts that continued into the 1 980s focusing primarily on development of a chemosterilant for wild stallions. The primary hormonal agent tested, testosterone propionate, was found to be effective in reducing sperm motility and effectively sterilizing the wild stallions for up to six months (Garrott and Siniff 1992). The hormone did not affect libido of the stallions, but foal production was reduced 83% in harems with treated stallions compared to those with untreated stallions (Kirkpatrick and Turner 1982).

There were a number of drawbacks to use of the hormonal sterilant. Application required immobilization of the stallion and injection of a large dose of the agent. A dose consisted of 2.5 - 10.0 g of a long-acting form of testosterone propionate, encapsulated in a biodegradable, nontoxic lactide coating to prolong the release of the hormone over a four to six month period. Additionally, (1) foaling times in treated herds shifted into the summer or fall (Garrott and Siniff 1992); (2) herding, capturing, immobilizing and injecting the harem stallions on an annual basis was difficult and costly; (3) long-term effects on the treated horses remained unknown; and (4) it was believed the agents could enter the food chain. For these reasons, chemical sterilization of stallions was abandoned as a focus for research into fertility control.

Silicone Implants in Mares

Silicone rods impregnated with progesterone and estradiol were implanted into the necks of mares and blocked ovulation for up to 28 months (National Research Council 1991). This work was also suspended because the invasive nature of the surgery and the unacceptable stress placed on mares.

The PZP Investigations

The scientific community identified the needs for an ideal fertility control agent in 1991 as follows (Kirkpatrick and Turner 1991; Seal 1991):

1) The agent should be at least 90% effective.
2) The agent should be capable of administration by remote delivery.
3) The agent should either be immediately reversible, or its effects should passively wear off.
4) The agent should be safe to pregnant animals.
5) The agent should not pass through the natural food chain.
6) The agent should be inexpensive.
7) There should be no debilitating side effects on the health of the horses.
8) The agent should not influence the social behavior of the horses.

This list of needs would drive much of the U.S. contraceptive research into wildlife species during the 1 990s, including research funded by both the BLM and the USGS-BRD. To meet the stated criteria, the National Park Service (NPS) research team on Assateague Island National Seashore turned to an immunocontraceptive agent, porcine zona pellucida (PZP), for the wild horses[3] on the island (Kirkpatrick and Turner 1982; Kirkland et al. 1992; Turner 2000; Kirkpatrick 1995), which had been reported to block fertilization in dogs, rabbits, and primates. In order for sperm to attach to the ovum and fertilize the egg, there must be complementary proteins on both the surface of the sperm and the zona pellucida (ZP) of the ovum. PZP is a foreign protein against which the treated mare produces anti-PZP antibodies. These antibodies attach to the mare's zonae sperm receptors on the ovum and block fertilization (Floorman and Wasserman 1985; Kirkpatrick 1995). Zona pellucida from domestic pig ovaries (obtained from slaughter houses) is minced and the PZP is obtained from screening filtration. Freund's Complete Adjuvant (FCA) is mixed with the PZP in order to enhance its effects when it is initially injected into mares intramuscularly.

Experimental PZP application on the wild horses of Assateague Island began in 1988. Following promising reductions in the pregnancy rates in mares (Kirkpatrick 1985; Kirkpatrick et al. 1990), the NPS in 1994 began to stabilize the growth of the population solely using PZP immunocontraception (Kirkpatrick and Turner, in press). The Assateague research team also developed non-invasive methods to assess the pregnancy rates of, and detect ovulation in, free- ranging treated and non-treated mares by analyzing reproductive steroid metabolites in feces and urine (Kirkpatrick et al. 1992). These methods require the sample be taken in the field from individually recognizable mares, but no captures are necessary.

It is impossible in this report to do justice to the larger volume of research conducted on PZP in wild horses on both western rangelands and on the eastern national seashores. Instead, we direct the reader to the summary papers of the J. Turner/J. Kirkpatrick/I. Liu research team (Kirkpatrick et al. 1992; Kirkpatrick 1995; Turner et al. 2000; Kirkpatrick and Turner, in press; Turner and Kirkpatrick, in press), to review the papers of Kreeger (1997) and Curtis and Warren (1999) and to annual reports of the research study (Turner et al. 1993 through 2001). Copies of these reports may all be obtained by writing to the National Program Office, Wild Horse and Burro Program, Reno Nevada.

The Outlook for PZP

The PZP agent appears to meet most of the safety concerns of the BLM: it does not enter the food chain, its effects passively wear off with time if the injections are terminated, normal reproduction can be resumed, following up to seven years of use, and it does no harm if injected into mares that are already pregnant — they carry foals to term. Initial research suggests native PZP does not affect ovarian function, hormonal health, or safety in pregnant animals (Turner et al. 1999, 2000; J. Turner, personal communication, Nov. 26, 2001). Life span and health of treated mares may be increased, apparently due to the absence of stresses from pregnancy and lactation. Treated mares apparently live about five to ten years longer than do untreated mares that continue to get pregnant and produce young (Kirkpatrick and Turner 2002). One initial study suggested harem behaviors are not influenced (Powell 1999). There appear to be no generational effects — offspring of treated mares are able to reproduce normally (Kirkpatrick and Turner, in press; Turner and Kirkpatrick, in press). The agent is about 90% effective in blocking fertility in mares.

Best results using PZP are achieved following an initial "primer" dose, followed by annual "booster" shots. The initial injection, or primers, may be administered to mares following gathers when they are in chutes during capture. Alternatively, in those populations where the individual mare can be both recognized and approached on foot for darting, the injection may also be administered remotely by means of a 1.0cc dart with a Pneu-bait or Dan-Inject dart gun. A second booster shot is then required for each year of immunocontraception. Following the second or third year of treatments, only an every-other or every-third year booster is needed (J. Kirkpatrick, pers. comm.). Following cessation of the annual treatments, the agent and the antibodies passively decline, anti-fertility effects wear off, and normal reproductive function is resumed the subsequent year. However, following seven or more years of treatment, the antifertility effects may be permanent for individual mares (Kirkpatrick and Turner 2002).

PZP has been successfully applied to control fertility and limit the size of several small populations of wild horses on eastern barrier islands for periods of a few to 14 years (Assateague Island National Seashore, Cape Lookout National Seashore, Shackleford Banks; Carrot Island, Rachel Carson National Estuarine Reserve; and Little Cumberland Island, a private island). Progress is continuing on development of a time-release pellet vaccine of PZP that will allow two years (actually ~22 months) of fertility control with only a single shot injection (Turner et al. 1999, 2000, 2001). Progress on this time-release form is encouraging, although efficacy rates are variable and may be slightly lower (~ 85%) than for the conventional multiple injection program.

Two major drawbacks of conventional PZP and Time-Release PZP have been identified by BLM managers: (a) the brief duration – managers prefer a one-shot, three to five-year duration, and (b) the fact that the most effective known adjuvant, FCA, present some health concerns. While the one-year or two-year durations of these forms may be adequate, and even preferred for small populations of wild horses, managers of the larger herds, such as herds in Nevada and Wyoming, have a critical need for a single application agent that lasts longer. If a gather is held during the summer or early fall, and the Time-Release PZP is injected, only one effective season of contraception maybe achieved. Also, some mares could become pregnant late during the second subsequent summer. There are some concerns about a lower survival of late born foals.

The BLM's long-term management needs clearly include both a shorter duration agent for small herds and a longer duration agent for the largest herds. A high priority of this research plan is to develop either a further time release extension of PZP, or develop a new agent that meets this need for a single-dose, longer duration contraceptive. In response to these needs BLM has just implemented a long-term study with captive wild horse mares to test the safety and efficacy of a newly-developed 3-4 year PZP vaccine.

BLM also seeks an alternative adjuvant to FCA. FCA can cause health problems when used in horses and following accidental injection or needle stick in people. FCA causes a false positive TB test, and can cause granulomas at injection sites in treated mares. These are generally small and shrink over time when the injection is into the buttock area of the horse. Presently, these risks are mitigated by only allowing persons trained and certified to administer the PZP and FCA mixture. These individuals must carefully following administration protocols in the field. Zoo Montana has trained BLM specialists in the past to handle the PZP and FCA mixture. However, a safer alternative adjuvant is desired. Modified Freund's Adjuvant (MFA) and other adjuvants may be potential replacements. Preliminary results from a recent study comparing the efficacy and duration of MFA as a replacement are encouraging and suggest that MFA may be an effective replacement for FCA with wild horses. BLM will substitute a new adjuvant as soon as an effective replacement for FCA can be identified.

One intriguing new candidate agent form of PZP is referred to as SpayVac™. It is simply PZP, combined with a FDA-approved adjuvant, incorporated within or between several layers of multi-lamellar liposomes. The liposome technology was developed by a team of scientists headed up by Dr. Robert Brown of Dalhousie University, Nova Scotia. The patent is held by Dr. Brown and Mark Fraker of Terramar Environmental Research Ltd., Vancouver, B.C. The liposome technology effects are not completely understood, but in one study using harbor seals, titers to the agents remained high following a single dose and pregnancy was blocked for more than eight years in the female seals (Brown et al. 1997). One big advantage of SpayVac™ is that its main component is PZP, and thus, many PZP research results should also apply. Although the duration of SpayVac™ is thought to be dose dependent (Lowell Miller, APHIS, May 2003, pers.corres), how long the effect will last, whether the duration will qualify SpayVac™ for use by the BLM, and whether the duration of contraceptive effects can be modified by altering the current liposome mixtures are questions that remain to be answered.

II. Overview of the Issues

A. Health and Handling Issues

The BLM gathers and holds in facilities wild horses and burros for periods of weeks to several months prior to adoption. In some cases if animals are determined to be unadoptable, they may be held for several years in long-term pasture holding facilities. During these pre-adoption and long term holding periods, the animals are under the care and supervision of the BLM. Health care includes multiple inoculations against pathogens, hoof trimming as needed, and de-worming on a regular basis. The animals are wild, handling creates some stress and they may be injured during handling, transport or treatment activities. Animals are also concentrated in the facilities, and infectious diseases can rapidly pass through the animals.

The BLM seeks to minimize the stress of handling and use the most effective and cost efficient health management practices available to safeguard the health and well-being of the animals under their care. Research is needed to identify optimal handling and healthcare practices that are not completely understood at this time because of the distinct differences between wild and domestic equids and the unique challenges associated with the large facilities in which they are managed.

Health problems among free roaming wild horses and burros are uncommon. Most of the health research needs of the free roaming wild horse and burro populations under BLM management are limited to better understanding how to manage emergency situations related to severe range conditions and how range conditions influence the health of animals at the time they are gathered. The need to support research to improve our understanding of the health of wild horses and burros on- and off-the-range is recognized in the context of the overall strategic plan for wild horse and burro research.

B. Fertility Control in Wild Horses[4]

Fertility control cannot be used to reduce herds of wild horses that are substantially over AML, or alone to limit population growth. Fertility control will assist the gather and removal program in achieving these two goals. The BLM seeks two fertility control agents, or two forms of the same agent that will reduce the frequency and/or size of expensive gathers and removals, and that will reduce the number of animals that will need to be removed from the range and adopted. The BLM seeks a shorter-term duration agent that will provide two years of contraception following a single injection for safe management of smaller herds of wild horses where population viability is a concern. The current form of Time-Release PZP may meet the need of the short-term agent, pending the results of the planned field trials. For larger herds of wild horses, the BLM seeks a contraceptive agent that lasts three to five years following a single injection. Gathers occur on a four-year cycle. Contraceptive management could focus on young to prime-aged mares following genetic guidance (Gross 2000). These mares could be injected once with an agent with a four-year duration, thus contracepted for four years, but then be allowed to passively return to fertility and contribute genetically for the remainder of their lives. A new group of young or prime-aged mares would be treated at the next four-year gather.

FCA is the most tested, most efficacious, and the best available adjuvant at this time. However, recent studies suggest the agencies should expand the search for a new adjuvant.

There are concerns that FCA could cause some health problems. The BLM is working to replace FCA with another adjuvant, such as MFA, as soon as possible.

Sufficient prior work with PZP has been conducted on wild horses in Nevada and on Assateague Island to justify field trails at this time. However, significant unanswered questions remain concerning population and behavioral effects of the treatments that must be addressed before BLM proceeds with broad-scale management applications of fertility control.

Development of a new agent, or further time-release development of PZP, may follow one of two different paths. First, the BLM may pursue the path of Food and Drug Administration (FDA) approval of the agent. Full commercial development of the agent may be necessary, to defray costs of the approval process. A commercial company could produce the agent for purchase by the BLM within their wild horse and burro program. The amount of agent needed annually by the BLM is too small alone to elicit much commercial interest. For example, it is estimated one person in a few weeks time can produce all of the PZP that would be needed by the BLM to control wild horses each year. If the agent was also useful for other purposes (e.g., spaying of dogs, cats, or livestock) perhaps commercial interest might occur. This process can be time consuming and expensive (e.g., several million dollars), FDA approval of all safety, health, and efficacy work (Good Laboratory Practice and Good Clinical Practice guidelines must be followed) must occur, and the FDA must approve the final product. Approval of agents that already have prior usage and prior approval in domestic food animals, however, might be within the realm of possibility for the BLM. Second, the BLM may continue to use PZP or other new products under a research protocol. The BLM has selected this latter option for now for reasons of practicality and costs, although commercial development still remains an option at any time down the road. Third, the BLM may seek a legislative, non-investigational exemption for use of the current PZP mixture.

Reproduction in wild horses may differ in a number of subtle ways from domestic horses, for example, in the season of estrus cycles. The explanation for these observed differences may be merely environmental, or there may be some minor physiological differences that are inherited. Until the differences can be defined, the BLM has determined that non-invasive research into fertility control could be conducted on captured wild horses held in BLM facilities or with free roaming wild horses under the Fertility Control Field Trial Plan.

Fertility control is not as immediate and pressing a need in wild burros, as it so clearly is with wild horses. The social structure of burros, which lacks stable harem breeding units, combined with year-round breeding; would prove challenging for application of the current PZP technology. However, this challenge should not prevent the BLM from pursuing a solution to fertility control in wild burros. Given the limited financial resources available for fertility control research, it should be pursued in wild burros just as soon as some successes can be achieved with wild horses.

C. Population Estimation and Modeling

Wild horse and burro populations increase at a high annual growth rate and these high growth rates can be sustained annually for many years. Active management programs are required for wild horses and burros that include detailed tracking of population sizes, population growth rates, sex and age composition, and modeling of options for removal strategies and population goals.

Accurate population estimates for planning and management activities are essential. The management applications of either removal or contraception (or a combination of both) are based on the number of animals to be reduced and the intervals between management; however, these goals are only as accurate as the population estimate. Wild horse and burro managers need accurate and defensible aerial surveys.

A user-friendly computer model and manual has been developed to simulate the growth rate and long-term planning of management removals for wild horses (Jenkins 1996). Managers are in need of a similar model to simulate wild burro population dynamics and to plan removals. During aerial surveys made in the flat, treeless terrain of Nevada and Wyoming ~ 85% of the wild horses present are seen (Garrott et al. 1991). For aerial surveys over forested or tall shrub desert areas, there are no methods to determine the number of animals missed. One exception to this is the work of the Arizona Interagency Wild Burro Working Group, consisting of the BLM, State of Arizona, and other federal biologists. This group has developed aerial estimation techniques for wild burros in central Arizona with promising results.

D. Genetics

Although the current total number of wild horses in all the herds is very large (37,135 animals), the management goal for most herds is small. The BLM's stated AML goals are to manage 41% of the wild horse herds at a census number (N) of < 50 horses, and 54% of the herds at $N < 100$ horses. Genetic effective population size[5] for some of these herds may be set too low. At first glance, these statistics appear to be cause for concern.

Information is not available on how many of these small herds are truly isolated. If there was even occasional gene flow between two or more herds that resulted in at least one or two successful breeding animals every generation[6] that produced breeding offspring, then the genetic resources of all the groups would be maintained. Such groups of two or more subpopulations whose population dynamics are independent, but are connected by low levels of movements and gene flow, are referred to as a metapopulation. Clearly, many of the smaller wild horse populations are probably part of a larger metapopulation.

Inbreeding is apparently rare in wild horse populations. Horses in only a very small number (approximately 5) of the 203 HMAs have exhibited characteristics possibly attributable to inbreeding, such as cataract blindness, dwarfism, parrot-mouth, or club foot deformities. Most wild horse herds that have been sampled, exhibit moderate levels of genetic heterozygosity (both allozyme or biochemical and DNA heterozygosity) (Bowling and Touchberry 1990). Thus, there does not appear to be any immediate cause for concern about inbreeding depression[7] in wild horse herds.

Nonetheless, the committee recommended a cautious approach by the BLM. The agency should monitor for signs of inbreeding via conducting genetic surveys; monitoring genetic information and key indicators of genetic health; and estimating N_e, in a representative sample of herds (about five should be adequate). High inbreeding coefficients, and any bottlenecks[8], or losses of genetic heterozygosity are a cause for concern. However, research is still needed to determine optimal goals for genetic heterozygosity that will maintain the fitness of horses in the wild herds and prevent inbreeding depression.

E. Habitat Assessment and Setting Population Goals

Central to the BLM's management of wild horses and burros is the habitat evaluation process that the BLM specialists use to set the appropriate stocking numbers of wild horses, burros, domestic livestock, and any native grazers, such as elk or bighorn sheep. For wild horses and burros, this numeric goal is the AML. Equally important is the monitoring program that the BLM uses to determine the success of these various AMLs in protecting soil, vegetation, and wildlife resources of the area.

In 1988, the Department of the Interior's Board of Land Appeals decided that the wild horse and burro stocking levels and livestock numbers be set to achieve a "thriving natural ecological balance" for each herd management area. As noted earlier, the Federal Land Policy and Management Act of 1976, the Public Rangelands Improvement Act of 1978, and orders from Congress have directed the BLM to manage the number of wild equids to accommodate multiple uses of other resources and the long-term sustainability of the range.

Diverse methods have been used to set the AMLs on the BLM lands. Currently all offices are required to adhere to the Land Use Plan process to determine AMLs and livestock numbers, including public scooping, plan development, National Environmental Policy Act analysis, and information from on-going monitoring. But since state offices have the lead role in habitat assessments, there is some diversity in how the various states conduct habitat monitoring. The BLM directs specialists to use new monitoring data to update forage allocation decisions in an adaptive management approach.

The BLM has an ongoing need for the incorporation of most up-to-date research findings and new techniques into their habitat monitoring and habitat restoration programs. For example, a GIS-based habitat model for wild horses would be useful to many managers.

The sheer size, diversity, and complexity of the BLM's current program, however, mandates that an in-depth assessment of habitat research needs to be conducted by the BLM. Such a major assessment was beyond the scope of the 2001 effort. Additionally, habitat research needs were viewed by the BLM as less pressing than other research needs (at least in 20012002). Several changes and improvements are currently underway in how the BLM deals with all of their grazing management, including how livestock, wild horses', and burro's grazing is integrated. It was premature to propose any additional changes at this time. Habitat research is deferred until such an in-depth analysis can be conducted by the BLM.

III. THE STRATEGIC PLAN

A. Health and Handling Strategies

The Challenge

While they are generally considered hardy, wild horses and burros face new challenges following capture. Even under the best conditions, simply handling wild animals to move them from pen to pen, load them on trailers or administer preventive or therapeutic medications is stressful and includes some increased risk of injury. Physiologically, stress increases susceptibility to infectious disease. Captured animals may be naive to diseases that are common among domestic equids (e.g., strangles), and they are mixed in larger groups than are typical under rangeland conditions. The logistics of gather, preparation and adoption often include the repeated transportation of animals over long distances. These factors combine to create unique health and handling challenges for the wild horse or burro compared with their domestic cousins.

Safeguarding the health and welfare of wild horses and burros includes identifying the most effective, least stressful way of handling and preparing them for their transition into captivity. A clean bill of health is also an important part of successful adoptions.

Most of the health research needs for wild horses and burros on-the-range are related to better understanding the health problems that occur in free ranging wild horses and burros. These are usually the direct or indirect result of man's influence (i.e., domestic horses exposing wild horses to infectious disease) or unusually harsh range conditions (e.g., drought, fires, plant toxicities).

Issues

1) Animals are placed in stressful circumstances during handling and transport from one holding facility to another, and illness and injuries may occur.

2) Infectious upper respiratory disease, including strangles and streptococcus zooepidemicus infection, occurs in animals in some facilities; and the sources of these infections are not known.
3) Record keeping concerning mortalities, nonfatal illness or injury, and medical and preventative treatments used at different facilities needs improvement.
4) Wild burros are unique and may have unique health problems (e.g., susceptibility to hyperlipemia and hyperinsulinema) and can become ill if moved too rapidly to areas with very different climates.
5) Optimal vaccination strategies and protocols to prevent certain infectious diseases (e.g., strangles, equine influenza, and herpes) and the effects of handling stress are not well understood.
6) We need a better understanding of how to best intervene when animals are acutely or chronically exposed to extreme range conditions brought on by drought or fire including water deprivation, starvation, and plant toxicities.
7) Incident clusters of plant toxicity (e.g., astragalus species), congenital or developmental abnormalities (e.g., parrot mouth, club foot) and unusual illness or death loss may need to be investigated on the range.
8) We need a better understanding of how subclinical conditions (e.g., nutritional deficiency, plant toxicity) impact immunocompetence and how animals cope with stress after removal
9) Procedures for blood banking need to be developed (also a recommendation of the WH&B Advisory Board) and implemented throughout the program.
10) There is no standard procedure for requesting, receiving, evaluating, and funding new research proposals. Unsolicited proposals should not drive the process. The BLM's needs should drive the process for research priority setting and calls for proposals.

Goals

11) Optimize preparation and health maintenance protocols to maintain, protect and improve the health and well being of wild horses and burros held in captivity.
12) Maintain safety for both the animals and persons involved during handling.
13) Be receptive to opportunities for improving handling procedures for wild horses and burros so they are better, and more efficient.
14) Better understand the health problems that occur in free ranging horses and how these problems may impact their health after removal.
15) Improve the adoptability of the wild horses and burros, and provide the public with animals that are healthier at the time of adoption, have lower rates of exposure to infectious disease and fewer health problems after adoption.

Strategies

The need for research to improve our understanding of the health needs of wild horses and burros on- and off-the-range is recognized in the context of the overall strategic plan for wild horse and burro research. This includes considering the impact of all research efforts (contraceptives, habitat evaluation, population modeling, etc.) on animal health and supporting research efforts aimed more specifically at animal health. Topics considered top priorities for health research include:

1) Consider additional research into the types of stress and injury that occur in wild horses and burros, their causes, and the best methods to reduce them during the transport. For example, identifying specific feed or trailer specifications that will minimize stress and injuries, and developing a better understanding of how electrolyte levels can be maintained during transport would be helpful.
2) Review the need for additional research on infectious upper respiratory diseases at holding facilities, identify sources of these infectious and ways to reduce the incidence of disease and impact on the program.
3) Develop a new more detailed monitoring system for mortalities and non-fatal illness and injury, as well as therapeutic and preventive treatments within facilities.
4) Research to better understand the incidence, causation, and prevention of diseases specific to wild burros.
5) Evaluate the effectiveness of vaccination strategies for strangles, equine influenza, herpes, and other diseases in stressed horses.
6) Review the need for investigating new gelding procedures, including the potential for injections of agents such as those that act against GnRH (Gonadotropin Releasing Hormone).
7) Develop and implement procedures for the safe, efficient banking of blood samples to facilitate animal health monitoring as a tool for improving animal health management (e.g. the emerging threat of West Nile virus infection).
8) Establish a standardized procedure for requesting, receiving, reviewing and funding health research proposals. The review procedure should include consideration of the scientific merits of the proposal as well as possible management implications for the BLM.
9) Use reviews of recent state-of-the-art research from the veterinary literature to address some of the Program's health research needs where possible. Make this information more readily available to specialists and thus, meet some information needs within the WH&B Program without the need for original research.

Other health problems and factors that are worthy of investigation in free roaming herds include problems or developmental abnormalities that may be related to nutritional deficiencies, plant toxicities or genetics, the unique attributes of wild horses that distinguish them from their domestic cousins (e.g., exceptional hoof quality), and monitoring wild horse and burro populations for infectious diseases that also impact the domestic horse population (e.g., vesicular stomatitis, equine infectious anemia).

Proposed Outcomes

1) Minimize transportation stress and injuries.
2) Reduce or eliminate incidence of upper respiratory diseases at some facilities.
3) A new health monitoring system for wild horses and burros.
4) Improve health of wild burros and reduce mortality and incidence of serious illness that result from the special needs of burros.

5) Ensure the most up-to-date and efficient vaccination strategies are available to the program.
6) Identify the most humane, effective and efficient gelding procedures.
7) Increase availability of blood banking procedures for all blood samples taken.
8) A program for objective and fair calls for review, and funding of proposals.
9) Review all research proposals for their potential impact on animal health.

B. Fertility Control in Wild Horses - Strategies

The Challenge

No single fertility control agent or device is currently available that meets all of the stated needs of the BLM. Contraceptive agents or physical devices are currently available that meet many of the stated goals. Both Conventional PZP and Time-Release PZP technology meet more of BLM's needs than any other tested known agent. Although significant questions remain concerning population-level treatment and behavioral effects, both Conventional and Time-Release PZP are ready for field trial testing in wild populations under a research protocol. A longer-lasting agent is needed for larger herds to provide contraception with a single dose. New adjuvants need to be tested as potential replacements for FCA. Even as research continues and new management programs are instituted, the USGS-BRD and the BLM must remain alert to any additional, potentially promising new developments and new agents. The BLM and USGS-BRD should not immediately abandon any ongoing work with PZP until a significantly better agent, or better form of the existing PZP agent, is developed and tested.

Issues

1) Over the next five years, the BLM plans to lower populations of wild horses and burros to levels more compatible with a healthy range in order to (1) improve the condition and survival of the wild equids and other wildlife, and (2) protect soil and vegetation resources.
2) This goal is nearly impossible to obtain with removals and adoptions alone. The current existing adoption process cannot handle the 10,000 animals gathered annually during the last few years. There are limitations of both facilities and demand by the public to adopt animals.
3) Trade-offs between a fertility control agent's effective duration, cost, and risk of population over-management have not been quantitatively explored. The BLM needs to know the implications of variable durations of agent(s) on their program. Are two agents clearly needed — one with short-term duration for small populations and one with longterm effects for larger populations?
4) To understand the effects of any stress due to handling for contraception.

Goals

1) Research should, as soon as possible, provide an effective fertility control tool to BLM for management use with wild horse mares that: (1) can be administered with a single injection; (2) is effective for multiple years; (3) is safe if administered to pregnant mares;
2) (4) is immediately reversible or passively wears off after which completely normal fertility and pregnancy in the mare can resume; (5) can be practically administered either remotely to habituated free-ranging wild animals or injected into animals held in facilities or restrained by equipment such as standard capture chutes; (6) will not enter the food chain; (7) can be tested under an INAD permit, or in the remote possibility of commercial interest, could eventually earn FDA approval; and (8) is greater than 90% effective in blocking pregnancy. At present, two forms of PZP – Conventional (multi-injection, one- year) and Time-Release (one-injection, two-year) –meet all of these criteria with one major exception; these forms do not meet the stated one-shot, three to five-year duration need of the BLM. Even the current Time-Release form needs some modification. Time- release PZP pellets made by either a heat-extrusion or a cold-evaporation process need to be evaluated. Beginning in 2002, field-trial tests were initiated with the currently available PZP agents. These will continue until a longer-lasting agent can be developed or becomes available. The purpose of these field trials is to provide the necessary information and assurances on population-level and behavior effects so that broad scale management of herds by PZP may proceed.
3) Develop a longer-lasting (three to five, or more, years) agent, or further modify and extend Time-Release PZP to achieve the one-shot, three to five-year need of the BLM. A longer-lasting agent must be developed and tested by the USGS-BRD and the BLM. Even a one-year extension of the current Time-Release form to a three-year duration would make a huge savings of efforts and costs for managers of larger herds. Given the fact that many gathers (and thus, the injections) would occur during the summer or early fall, the current two-year time-release form only provides contraception for one full breeding season. Even two breeding seasons of fertility control may be too brief for most herd managers since most gathers are on a three- or four-year cycle. In light of this, BLM initiated a test of a 3-4 year PZP vaccine with captive wild mares in March 2005.
4) Test alternative adjuvants to FCA that do not result in any false positive TB tests and are less objectionable. Test MFA, QS-21, and other adjuvants that would be less objectionable than FCA. A 10-month trail did occur with MFA in captive wild mares and was completed in October 2004. MFA is now being considered as an acceptable substitute to FCA. BLM will consider the replacement of FCA with MFA in all subsequent captive and field trials as the adjuvant to be used with PZP.

Strategies

1) Conduct preliminary modeling for direction and guidance on the numbers, age classes, and durations of treatments. — Model the tradeoffs, cost-benefits, and risks of the various durations of an agent. Based on this analysis, the BLM should then

select the optimum duration(s) for agents that they desire to use. Modeling should also guide the optimum mix of strategies (all contraception, all removal, or best mix of both), scenarios of marking, monitoring, handling, and mare selection (all young, random) to produce the greatest benefits to handlings and animals removed, to meet BLM's stated objectives for population viability. This preliminary modeling began in 2002, and is being done by researchers at Colorado State University. In addition, an economic analysis evaluating different management strategies with fertility control was modeled by John Bartholow, a BRD-USGS researcher, and completed in 2004.

2) Immediately conduct field tests with both Conventional PZP and Time-Released PZP under a research protocol until a longer-lasting agent is developed (Figure 2). Conduct research on the effects of PZP contraception on wild horse population growth rates, seasonality of foaling, any health complications, and any effects on behavior, and harem dynamics so that the information and assurances are available prior to proceeding with any broad-scale management application of PZP. Conduct those studies on wild horses in captivity for those topics where free-ranging wild horses cannot be observed with enough regularity (e.g., studies of effects on annual estrus cycling, studies of any complications). Population and individual-based studies, using conventional and time- release PZP, were initiated in 2002 and 2003 under the guidance of the Fertility Control Field Trial Plan.
3) Organize a competitive call for proposals to develop a longer-lasting agent.
4) Preliminary laboratory work with mixtures and dosages should occur by the developers, proponents and contractors.
5) Screen the safety of any new potential longer-lasting contraceptive agents first in captive settings before any testing in the field. Included in this listing are any new agents, adjuvants, and mixtures. Tests of FMA and a newly-developed 3-4 year PZP vaccine have been initiated with captive wild mare trials in 2004 and 2005, respectively.
6) Immediately start tests on the efficacy and duration of other adjuvants that are less objectionable and have a higher probability of FDA approval compared with FCA (e.g., Modified Freund's, QS-21)
7) Consider the potential for FDA-approvability in the selection of agents. If a longer-lasting (3-4 year) agent is developed, field trials on that agent should be immediately initiated.

The BLM has selected a two-pronged plan of attack to simultaneously: (1) aggressively pursue a final form of new agents or modification of currently available PZP that meets the longer-term duration needs, while also (2) aggressively field testing current PZP until any significantly better agent becomes available. Work on development and screening of new agents (Phase II) and field testing the best current agents (Phase III) should occur concurrently (Figure 2).

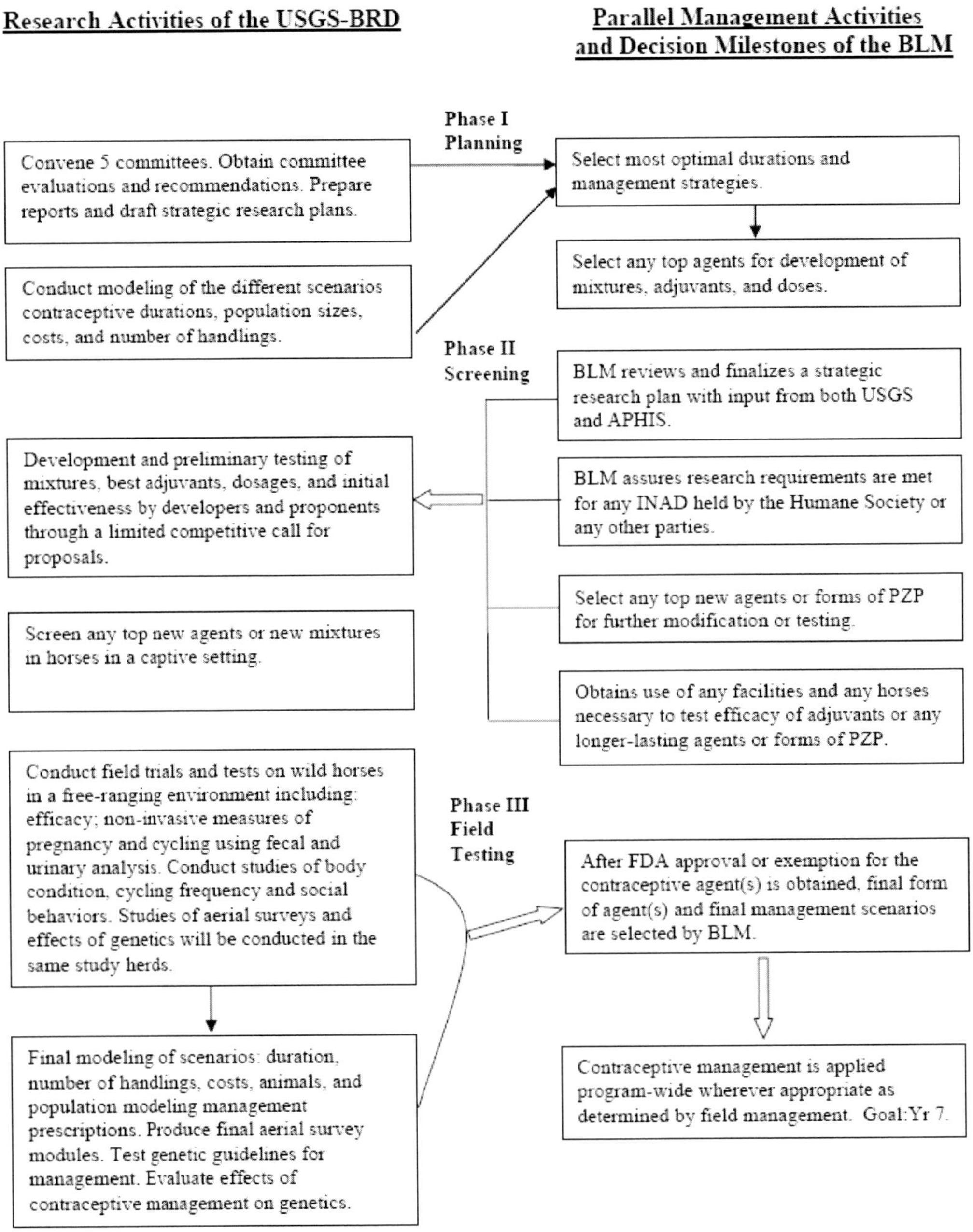

Figure 2. Project overview. Major research steps and corresponding decision milestones for the BLM are detailed.

The BLM and USGS-BRD initiated field tests with current PZP forms in 2002 and 2003, under the guidance of the Fertility Control Field Trial Plan. The respective agency research coordinators traveled to prospective study sites in 2002 and 2003 and visited with the herd area managers. Study sites were selected and field research initiated to obtain pre-treatment data wherever possible. Field studies started in 2002 and 2003, to run through 2007 and 2008, yielding one to two years of pretreatment data and four years of post-treatment data. Where pretreatment data collection was not possible, the controls to treated mares will be untreated mares in the same and in other harems. Research with aerial survey techniques and any field studies related to genetics should be conducted on these same study herds in order to maximize efficiency and save dollars. The field-trial research with PZP will also include the agent's effects on fertility control and body condition, studies on age-specific survival rates, harem organization and cohesion, duration of the breeding season, social behavior of mares, harem-tending behavior, and dominance relations among stallions.

Proposed Outcomes

1) A suitable, longer-lasting, and safe fertility control agent will be developed for consideration in broad-scale management application by the BLM. Fewer total animals will be rounded up and adopted. When lower maintenance population levels are reached, there will be longer intervals between gathers, and the gathers will be less expensive and smaller in scale. Fewer unadoptable animals will be held in long-term holding facilities at government expense.
2) Substantial savings in federal dollars will be accrued to the government. Presently, a large proportion of the entire budget of the WH&B Program is tied up in the enormous "Adoption Pipeline" – the process of gathering animals, holding them, transporting them, and then adopting them.
3) More stable populations will be achieved with contraceptive management than with the widely fluctuating current "increase-gather-increase" scenario. More genetic heterozygosity will be maintained and habitat will be protected under a more stable population scenario.
4) Fewer animals will be subjected to the stresses of capture and increased diseases and pathogen transmissions that go along with confinement of large numbers of animals.

C. Population Estimation and Modeling of Population Management Prescriptions – Strategies

The Challenge

The stated goal for the BLM's Wild Horse and Burro Program is to conduct a population census[9] or estimate on every herd area every four years, or more frequently if necessary. A few of the smallest, most accessible, and most visible of the wild horse herds may be completely censused using ground surveys, with identification based on photographs or unique natural markings of animals. Because wild burros possess fewer unique markings, identification systems do not appear to be possible for wild burros. The size of all burro herds and most wild horse herds are estimated from an aircraft, typically a helicopter. Wild horses in flat, treeless terrain are easily counted and it is estimated that ~ 85% of animals are seen. But, wild horses and burros may be missed in more rugged terrain and tree cover. Wild horse and burro specialists need standardized, tested, cost effective, defensible, yet easy-to-use aerial population estimation techniques for wild burro herds found in rugged and forested areas. The best technique(s) presented to the BLM wild horse managers in a format such as a computer diskette or CD-rom with easy-to-follow directions and a user manual. Some areas to be surveyed are so vast BLM managers may decide to count only portions of a herd area to save time and dollars. Stratified, random subsampling procedures may be used to obtain a valid estimate of the population size for these larger herds.

Issues

1) Aerial and ground population survey requirements for the BLM are daunting. The BLM is responsible for the management of over 200 wild horse and burro populations located across vast expanses of public lands.
2) In order to plan any management removals, the BLM requires population estimates, sex and age classification data, and population management modeling (Jenkins 1996) every three years on every herd area.
3) Sightability for wild burros is lower due to their small size, often cryptic colors, small groups (sizes are often single individuals), and stoic behavior. This results in many animals standing still as aircraft pass the rugged, brushy or riparian-forested habitats that they reside in. Sightability for burros from a helicopter may only be 40-60% of the animals present.
4) Wild horses are visible in flat, treeless terrain, but where patches of conifer cover are present, the estimated sightability of wild horses may be as low as one-half the animals present. Even in the more open terrain in Nevada, earlier scientific estimates of the percent of all wild horses observed are still only 66 to 85%.

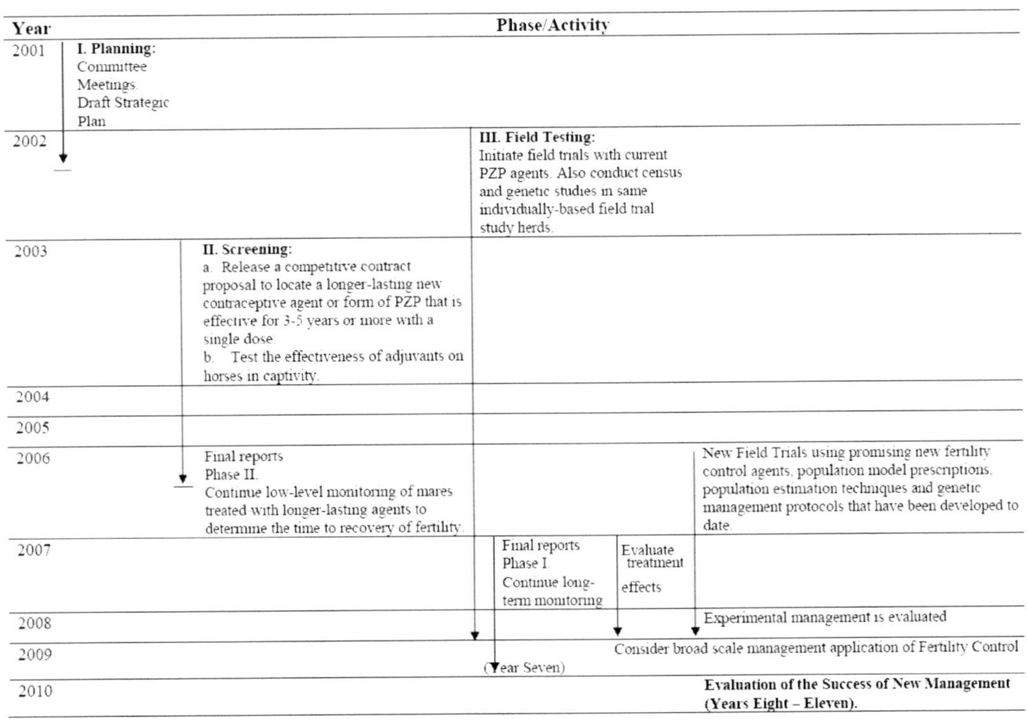

Figure 3. Phases I-II of the Strategic Research Plan for Wild Horses and Burros.

5) Cost, personnel, and fatigue factors may make aerial surveys of large areas prohibitive. Representative samples of these vast areas can be surveyed using stratified, random sampling, thus reducing the total area that needs to be surveyed. The BLM has directed the protocol include the option for subsampling, using these procedures.

Goals

1) To provide aerial and ground population estimation techniques for wild horses and burros that are valid, tested, defensible, cost-effective, easy to use, and that allow managers to survey representative reproductive subsamples of vast areas to obtain valid population estimates. Testing on several recommended techniques began in 2004.
2) To explore high resolution Department of Defense imagery as a possible substitute for helicopter surveys, if the technology was made available to the BLM.
3) To improve, update, and apply current population and genetic models to guide removal, genetic and contraceptive management needs.

Strategies

1) Develop aerial technique(s) and product(s) from amongst four candidates (Idaho Sightability Model, Simultaneous Double-Count, Distance Sampling, and Noninvasive Mark-Resight) for wild horses. Many wild horse herd management areas are managed for small populations that may be more amenable to mark-resight techniques using individually identifiable horses, and representative ground or aerial surveys of the area. Focus on development of those least invasive techniques that: (a) require no collaring or capture of wild horses, (b) only one aerial or ground survey per population estimate to minimize overflights and disturbances of the animals, and (c) allow subsampling.
2) Explore the availability of Department of Defense (DOD) satellite imagery for identification of horses as a potential substitute to helicopter surveys in some areas. However, the war on terrorism may make this imagery less available for the next few years.
3) Continue to monitor the progress of the Arizona Wild Burro Interagency Aerial Survey Working Group to develop a technique for wild burros. Currently the group is testing the Simultaneous Double-Count technique, with excellent initial success. Respond if the group asks for additional work or assistance. The need for wild burro aerial survey techniques will be addressed following the wild horse work.
4) Three population models have been developed for management application, all of which received high marks for performance by this and earlier panels. These models should continue to be updated and improved. In particular, the Jenkins population-removal model (Jenkins 1996) that is used by wild horse and burro specialists, is currently being revised for use with WINDOWS, and will include density dependence —both are significant improvements. The Gross model (Gross 2000) is excellent for modeling genetics and management scenarios. The Hobbs Model (Hobbs et al. 2000) is excellent for modeling contraceptive scenarios — but both models need updating with new research information.

Proposed Outcomes

1) Improved methods for population estimation will result in aerial surveys in herd management areas that are less expensive, more efficient and provide accurate estimates with confidence intervals on the estimates.
2) The techniques will be accessible by all wild horse and burro specialists.
3) The Jenkin's population model that the BLM currently uses will be improved.
4) Population models will be applied to more management questions concerning genetics and fertility control treatment plans.
5) DOD satellite imagery could substitute for helicopter surveys. Considerable cost savings could occur as could reduction in safety hazards to BLM personnel, if this imagery could be made available.

D. Genetic Conservation Strategies

The Challenge

BLM is mandated to manage for self-sustaining populations of wild horses and burros. Inbreeding appears rare in wild horses and burros. Genetic problems due to inbreeding depression, however, may be encountered in a few small, isolated populations of wild horses or wild burros. The BLM needs to guard against potential inbreeding problems by conducting surveys, as needed, of the genetics of wild horses and monitoring key indicators of heterozygosity, inbreeding coefficients, and genetic effective population sizes so that management intervention may be proactive.

Some potentially unique groups and phenotypes of wild horses occur on the BLM lands. The public recognizes these unique groups, particularly a few herds with Spanish colonial heritage. Existing genetic evidence supports the presence of early colonial Spanish horse alleles in some herds. This suggests these herds are more similar to early Spanish founder stock. However, wild horses possess no unique alleles that are not already found in domestic horses. Nothing in the 1971 Act or in policy, however, directs the BLM to provide special management for some groups of horses. The genetic and heritable components of any possibly unique traits, or unique groups of wild horses, should be tested during a comprehensive analysis of common ancestries amongst the herds. Similar or closely related herds of horses should be identified for any genetic augmentation of wild horse herds.

Issues

1) Population goals for some wild horse and burro herds may be too low to meet conventional standards for minimum genetically viable sizes (K. Schoenecker and F. Singer 1999. USGS-BRD report, Ft. Collins, CO). This is not a matter of immediate concern since many of these herds may have gene flow to other herds, thus forming a metapopulation. Even very limited gene flow (e.g., one to two breeding animals every generation) between subpopulations will guard against inbreeding. Wild horse herds were larger in the recent past, peaking in numbers about 1980. Thus, genetic concerns are a fairly recent issue. Only approximately five herds have produced

animals with physical defects. In only one of these cases was there sufficient background information on the herds' size and genetics to implicate inbreeding as the likely cause of the problems. Inbreeding may have caused the other problems, but they may also have been due to inherited defects.

2) Managers lack data on which herds are genetically isolated. Those herds need to be identified that possess low values of heterozygosity, and where severe bottlenecks, or high levels of inbreeding occur.
3) Unique phenotypic, historical and wild types of horses may exist; however, the genetic basis for any potential uniqueness has never been quantified.
4) Wild horses may be more vulnerable than many mammals to inbreeding depression at low population levels due to: (1) a harem breeding structure that limits breeding males mostly to harem holding stallions, and (2) a dominance hierarchy that usually delays harem holding and breeding in males until six to seven years of age or older.

Goals

1) Manage against inbreeding depression. Maintain healthy genetic fitness and viability of wild horses as a wildland species so they may survive and persist in unpredictable and often rigorous environments. Manage to minimize the need for augmentations, if possible.
2) Set minimum goals for genetic viability of the populations in terms of: (a) minimum levels of total heterozygosity (both allozyme and DNA), (b) minimum genetic effective population sizes, (c) maximum amounts of inbreeding, and (d) a maximum loss of alleles that will be allowed.
3) Identify any small[10] and truly isolated herds of wild horses through both genetic analysis and also reviews of the movements, herd histories, and sizes of the herds in question. Small and isolated herds are a cause of concern. Identify any metapopulations or collections of connected subpopulations where small size of some subpopulations will not be a concern.
4) Document any relatedness and any uniqueness of all the herds. Quantify relatedness amongst herds to guide any introductions of new animals. Establish prevalence and habitability of any special traits or phenotypes.
5) Establish management protocols for genetically "rescuing" small, isolated populations of wild horses through introductions of new individuals from genetically related or similar herds.
6) Conduct research on what is the minimum size for viable populations.

Strategies

1) Conduct a comprehensive survey of the genetics of all the wild horse populations. Determine which small wild horse herds, if any, are truly genetically isolated. Although
2) previous genetic blood draws were done on several herds, systematic surveys were initiated in 2003 whereby all herds subjected to population control gathers were also subjected to blood draws for genetic evaluation purposes. Reports are generated for

each herd identifying founder stock, level of diversity and management recommendations for avoiding inbreeding problems.

3) Determine the effects of contraception on rates of loss of herd heterozygosity.
4) Document the inbreeding genetic contribution, if any, to the deformities observed in a few specific herds. Develop guidelines for avoiding these situations in the future, and for avoiding deformities that have a genetic component.
5) Determine, through field studies, the threshold levels of heterozygosity and inbreeding below which reduced fitness and inbreeding depression may occur in wild horses, so that the BLM can avoid these situations.
6) Calculate genetically effective population sizes (Ne) in at least five populations of wild horses (two are already completed) so that the BLM will know the average and range of Ne to census N ratios to establish generality for minimum population sizes for viability.
7) Conduct a meta-analysis of the genetic information for all the herds. Conduct quantitative statistical analyses to identify the commonalities and relatedness of all the groups of wild horses. These commonalities may guide which herds are selected for the introduction of new animals. Additionally, the thresholds for management intervention need to be quantitatively assessed, defensible and published. Currently, the genetics contract only allows for sampling and analysis of individual herds
8) Search for any patterns in fitness lines, matrilines, patrilines, etc., that would alter the estimation of Ne/N. How managers select horses for removals vs. those left on the range to breed may alter genetics of the herd. Conduct an analysis of parentage, using DNA markers, in three individually-based study herds to accomplish this.
9) Identify meta-populations within each given area, region, or state.

Proposed Outcomes

10) Minimum guidelines and protocols will be established for management intervention to maintain fitness, avoid inbreeding depression, and prevent genetic defects due to inbreeding in wild horse herds. Key genetic parameters will be monitored.
11) There will be documentation of the genetic basis for the relatedness of groups to guide the introduction of new animals for genetic purposes to identify any unique traits or any unique groups of wild horses.

E. Habitat Assessment and Setting Population Goals

Deferred pending a more in-depth analysis of BLM's needs related to habitat assessment, monitoring and evaluation.

IV. GLOSSARY

a) *Adjuvants* - A component of the vaccine that enhances the main product, or antigen, and consequently increases antibody formation. Adjuvants can also delay the release of the vaccine as in the case of SpayVac. The vaccine works much more efficiently with the adjuvant. These are general immunostimulants that cause the body to make greater concentrations of antibodies against the vaccine.

b) *Appropriate Management Level (AML)* – The Wild and Free-Roaming Horse and Burro Act of 1971, the Taylor Grazing Act of 1934 and the Federal Land Policy and Management Act of 1976 all direct the BLM to set appropriate numbers of grazing animals, including wild horse and burros, and to manage for those goals, or AMLs. AML goals are determined through the BLM's planning process, and are later evaluated with monitoring at levels that will allow for healthy, self-sustaining populations of equids, a Thriving Natural Ecological Balance (TNEB), and are compatible with other uses.

c) *Chemosterilants* - This term broadly refers to any chemical agent that causes temporary or permanent sterility.

d) *Contraception* - A chemical or agent that prevents pregnancy in any manner, typically by blocking either ovulation or fertilization. Contraception is usually temporary. Fertility usually returns passively after treatment has been terminated.

e) *Fertility Control* - A collective term that refers to all methods of inhibiting reproduction.

f) *Immunocontraceptives* - Contraceptive agents stimulate the body's immune response in the host animal against hormones or proteins essential for reproduction, and in doing so blocks pregnancy or some other essential component of reproductive function. Immunocontraception may include vaccines directed at either reproductive hormones, at sperm, or at the ovum. Most wildlife applications include vaccines that are directed at blocking fertilization in the female by stimulating production of antibodies against the zona pellucida (ZP) of the ovum.

g) *Investigational New Animal Drug Exemption (INAD)* - A research permit issued by the U.S. Food and Drug Administration (FDA) for research into new or untested compounds including contraceptive agents. This permit is required for any new drug research with animals.

h) *Passive Return, Reversible and Permanent Fertility Control Agents* - Reversible fertility control agents as those agents whose antifertility effects can be immediately terminated with a reversing agent and normal reproductive function resumed. Immediate reversibility might include a reversing agent that is administered, or a physical device such as an IUD that can be removed and normal reproductive function returns. A reversible agent provides a number of advantages in that the number of animals returned to reproductive potential is immediately known. PZP is an example of the agents that, in the absence of an annual booster, normal reproductive function is passively resumed, as the effects of the agent wear off. The term permanent when applied to fertility control agents is also operationally vague. Except for the removal of the reproductive organs which permanently impair reproduction, the agents often referred to as permanent, such as GnRH-PAP, may be long-term but may not prove to be truly permanent.

i) *Physical Methods of Fertility Control: Intrauterine Devices (IUDs)* - Physical rings or other devices that are placed in the uterus and prevent pregnancy. This approach has been used to successfully block pregnancy in humans and in a large number of animal species, including six domestic horse mares (Daels and Hughes 1995). All of these mares produced foals following the removal of a O-ring shaped IUD. In humans, IUD's were demonstrated to be effective for as long as 12 years, at which time their effects were still reversible.

j) *Sterilization* - An inability to reproduce. Usually refers to a more or less permanent infertility, such as would occur by removal of male (castration, or the gelding process) or female reproductive organs (neutering, or spaying process). Several agents listed in this report mimic sterilization in the short term, or in some cases longer term, e.g., seven years, but none are felt to cause permanent sterility – some recovery of normal reproductive function is likely.

k) *Strangles* – Strangles is a highly contagious, infectious respiratory disease of equids caused by the bacterium *Streptococcus equi* subspecies *equi.* Characterized by inflammation of the upper respiratory tract infection often results in abscessation of intermandibular, parotid or pharyngeal lymph nodes. Immunologically naïve horses are at greater risk for infection and outbreaks often occur in large populations that have frequent additions. Although mortality is rare, morbidity can approach 100%. Immunization against *S. equi equi* does not always prevent infection, though it may prevent severe manifestations of disease in infected animals.

l) *Thriving Natural Ecological Balance (TNEB)* - The Wild and Free-Roaming Horse and Burro Act of 1971 requires that wild horses, burros and wildlife, be in good health and reproducing at a rate that sustains the population; the key vegetation is able to maintain its composition; the soil is being protected; and a sufficient amount of high quality water is available to all animals.

V. Literature Cited

Bennett, D. 1998. *Conquerors, the roots of New World horsemanship.* Amigo Publications, Solvang, California. 422 pp.

Bennett, D. and R.S. Hoffman. 1999. Equus caballus. *Mammalian Species* 628:1-14.

Bowling, A.T. and R.W. Touchberry. 1990. Parentage of Great Basin feral horses. *Journal of Wildlife Management* 54:424-429.

Brown, R.G., W.D. Bowen, J.D. Eddington, W.C. Kimmins, M. Mezei, J.L. Parsons, and B. Pohajdak. 1997a. Temporal trends in antibody production in grey harp and hooded seals to a single administration immunocontraceptive vaccine. *Journal of Reproductive Immunology* 35:53-64.

Brown, R.G., W.D. Bowen, J.D. Eddington, W.C. Kimmins, M. Mezei, J.L. Parsons, and B. Pohajdak. 1 997b. Evidence for a long-lasting single administrative contraceptive agent in wild grey seals. *Journal of Reproductive Immunology* 35:43-5 1.

Burnham, K.P., B. Pugesek, G.A. Sargeant, F.J. Singer, H.B. Underwood. B. Shanks (compiler). 2000. *USGS Review of Wild Horse Population Model,* USGS-BRD, Washington D.C. 2 pp.

Coughenour, M.B. 2000. *Ecosystem modeling of the Pryor Mountain Wild Horse Range.* Final Report to U.S. Geological Survey and Bureau of Land Management, Colorado State University, Fort Collins.

Curtis, P.D. and R.F. Warren. 1999. *A workshop on the status and future of wildlife fertility control.* The Wildlife Society, Washington, D.C.

Floorman, P.M. and H.M. Wasserman. 1985. O-linked oligosaccharides of mouse egg ZP3 account for its sperm receptor activity. *Cell* 41:313-324.

Garrott, R.A. and D.B. Siniff. 1992. Limitations of male-oriented contraception for controlling feral horse population. *Journal of Wildlife Management* 56:456-464.

Gross, J.E. 2000. A dynamic simulation model for evaluating effects of removal and contraception on genetic variation and demography. *Biological Conservation* 96:319-330.

Gross, J. P. McCue, L. Miller, O. Ryder and B.H. Underwood. (B. Shanks, compiler). 1999. Research evaluation: Contract for immunization/contraception and fertility in wild horses. *USGS-BRD Report to BLM.*

Hobbs, N.T., D.C. Bowden and D.L. Baker. 2000. Effects of fertility control on populations of ungulates: General, stage-structured models. *Journal of Wildlife Management* 64:473-491.

Holzgang, O. 1997. Herbivore – carrying capacity of grasslands in the Swiss National Park. *Thesis.* Swiss Federal Institute of Technology, Zurich.

Jenkins, S.H. 1996. *Wild horse population model, Version 3.2. Users Guide.* Department of Biology, University of Nevada, Reno.

Johnson, B.K., et al. 2001. Application of multi-species stocking allocation models to study herbivory in the interior West USA. *Paper presented at International Conference on Forest Dynamics and Ungulate Herbivory,* Davos, Switzerland, October 3-6, 2001.

Kirkpatrick, J.F. and J.W. Turner. 1982. *Reproductive biology and chemical fertility control in feral horses.* Final Report to BLM on Contract.

Kirkpatrick, J.F., J.W. Turner, Jr. 1991. Changes in herd stallions among feral horse bands and the absence of forced copulation and induced abortion. *Behavioral Ecology and Sociobiology* 29(3):217-219.

Kirkpatrick, J. 1995. Management of wild horses by fertility control: the Assateague experience. *NPS Scientific Monograph No. 26,* Denver Colorado.

Kirkpatrick, J.F., I.K.M. Liu, J.W. Turner Jr., and R. Keiper. 1992. Long term effects of porcina zonae pellucida immuno contraception on ovarian function of feral horses. *Journal of Reproduction and Fertility* 94:437-444.

Kirkpatrick, J.F., S.E. Shideler, and J.W. Turner Jr. 1990. Pregnancy determinations in uncaptured feral horses based on free steroids in feces and steroidal metabolites in urine-soaked snow. *Canadian Journal of Zoology* 68:2576-2579.

Kirkpatrick, J.F. and A. Turner. 2002 (in press). *Reversibility of action and safety during pregnancy in wild horses immunized against porcine zona pellacida.* Reproduction.

Kissell, R. Jr., L.R. Irby, and R.J. Mackie. 1996. *Competitive interactions among bighorn sheep, feral horses, and mule deer in Bighorn Canyon National Recreation Area and Pryor Mountain Wild Horse Range.* Completion report of the U.S. National Park Service. Montana State University.

Kreeger, T. editor. 1997. Contraception in Wildlife Management. USDA, Animal and Plant Health Investigation Service. *Technological Bulletin* 1853.

Little, D.K., K. Grissom, R. Oyler, C. Barnes, S. Elefritz, J. Christensen, G. Acheson, L. Thomas, J. Herrert, R. Lee, A. Fuller, M. Pierce, and S. Kohnke. 1999. *Report of the Arizona Burro Census Team.* BLM, Phoenix, Arizona.

Liu, I.K.M., M. Bernoco, M. Feldman. 1989. Contraception in mares heteroimmunized with pig zonae pellucidae. *Journal of Reproduction and Fertility.* 85:19-29.

National Research Council. 1982. Wild and free-roaming horses and burros. *Final Report.* National Academy Press, Washington, D.C.

National Research Council. 1991. *Wild horse populations: field studies in genetics and fertility.* National Academy Press, Washington, D.C. 42 pp.

Powell, D.M. 1999. Preliminary evaluation of porcine zona pellucida (PZP), immunocontraception for behavioral effects in feral horses (Equus caballus). *Journal of Animal Welfare Science* 2:321-335.

Schoenecker, K.A. and F.J. Singer. 1999. A survey of BLM wild horse managers to assess research needs. *Report to the BLM.* USGS, Midcontinent Ecological Science Center. 8 pp.

Smith, G., C. Bacomb, K. Estielman, D. Aicher, K. Harrison, and D. Little. 1996. *Report of the review team on forage allocation for wild horses and livestock.* USDI, Bureau of Land Management, Reno, NV. 37 pp.

Turner, J.W., Project Director. 1999, 2000, 2001, 2002. Annual Progress Reports on USDI-BLM Assistance Agreement. *Nevada Wild Horse Fertility Control Project.* Medical College of Ohio.

Turner, A. and J.F. Kirkpatrick. 2002 (in press). *Effects of immunocontraception on population, longevity and condition in wild mares* (Equus caballus). Reproduction.

Turner, C. L., T. R. Seastedt, and M. I. Dyer. 1993. Maximization of above ground grassland production: The role of defoliation frequency, intensity, and history. *Ecological Applications* 3:175–186.

United States Department of the Interior, Bureau of Land Management. 2000. Summary Recommendations – BLM Wild Horse and Burro Population Viability Forum, April 21, 1999. *BLM Resource Note No. 35,* BLM, National Science and Technology Center, Washington, D.C. 4 pp.

USDI, BLM. 1997. Summary Recommendations – BLM Wild Horse and Burro Population Viability Forum, *BLM National Resource Note No. 35,* National Science and Technology Center, BLM, Washington, D.C. 4 pp.

Wagner, F.H. 1983. Status of wild horse and burro management on public rangelands. *North American Wildlife and Natural Resources Conference* 48:116-133.

VI. Acknowledgements

The efforts of Linda Coates-Markle (BLM), Albert Kane (APHIS) in reviewing all sections of this plan are appreciated. Dr. Kane drafted the health sections and Francis Singer (BRD) the remaining sections. The help of Tom Pogacnik, John Fend, Bud Cribley (BLM), Lisa Hatcher (APHIS), and Sue Haseltine, Denny Fenn, Bernie Shanks, Doug Posson, Juliette

Wilson, Greg Smith, and Zachary Bowen (USGS-BRD) was invaluable to the planning process. Matt Tobler, Laurie Richards, and Jennifer Sunderland assisted with the many redrafts of this plan. The members of the five advisory committees greatly assisted this planning effort: The Health Committee: Katie Blunk, APHIS; Linda Coates-Markle, BLM; Ann Davidson, Louisiana State University; Ted Friend, Texas A&M University; Lisa Hatcher, APHIS; Albert Kane, APHIS; Sharon Kipping, BLM; Robin Lohnes, WHB Advisory Board; Rebecca McConnico, Louisiana State University; Mo Salman, CSU; Francis Singer, USGS; Mark Stewart, APHIS; Joe Stratton, BLM; Josie Traub-Dargatz, CSU; Bea Wade, BLM. The Genetics Committee: Linda Coates- Markle, BLM; Gus Cothran, University of Kentucky, Philip Hedrick, Arizona State University; Leonard Nunney, University of California; Sara Oyler, USGS; Bruce Pugesek, USGS; Rob Ramey III, Denver Museum Of Nature and Science; Dan Rubenstein, Princeton University; Philip Sponenberg, Virginia-Maryland College of Veterinary Medicine. The Contraceptives Committee: Lowell Miller, APHIS Co-chair; Dan Baker, Colorado Division of Wildlife; Linda Coates-Markle, BLM; Gary Killian, Pennsylvania State University; Patrick McCue, Colorado State University; Glen Sargeant, USGS; Mike Whitacre, University of North Carolina. The Population Committee: Linda Coates-Markle, BLM; E.O, Garton, University of Idaho; Kelly Grissom, BLM; Lisa Hatcher, APHIS; John Hervert, Arizona Game and Fish; Tom Hobbs, CSU; Steve Jenkins, University of Nevada; Bruce Lubow, APHIS; Glen Sargeant, USGS.

ENDNOTES

[1] Since no systematic surveys were conducted at this time, some authors feel this number may not be representative of the numbers in 1971.

[2] The committee reports may be obtained by accessing www.wildhorseandburro.blm.gov

[3] These animals are small horses, not ponies. Horses and ponies differ in several important ways, such as in length of gestation.

[4] The listing order of topics does not imply priorities of timing or funding. The BLM will establish timing and funding priorities on an annual basis following input from USGS-BRD and APHIS.

[5] Genetic effective population size (N_e) is a measure of the number of animals within a population that are not only breeding, but their progeny are successfully contributing their genes to the next generation. This complex topic is covered in more detail in Appendix II and III. N_e can be used to estimate the rate of loss of genetic heterozygosity (H_o) and loss of allelic diversity per generation in a population. The recommendation for $N_e > 50$ came from the breeders of domestic animals that found the level of loss acceptable. This number will result in a predicted loss of 1% of the heterozygosity (H) present per generation. The $N_e = 50$ rule may not be adequate for wild populations since selection pressures are more severe in the wild. N_e of larger than 50 may be required for wild species to adapt to more severe environmental conditions or changes. The N_e calculations assume random mating, which is never true with equids, and no mating of close relatives, which might not be the case in the smallest equid populations.

[6] A wild horse generation equals 5-14 years.

[7] Inbreeding depression is defined as the loss of fecundity or viability due to inbreeding. It can frequently manifest itself as a specific genetic defect in horses.

[8] A population bottleneck is defined as a short-term population reduction to a small size that may reduce genetic heterozygosity.

[9] A census is typically defined as a total count. Total counts are rarely possible, however, since animals are found in tree cover and dispersed over large areas of rough terrain. Thus, a population estimate with a confidence interval on that estimate is a more reasonable goal for managers.

[10] Small populations are defined as $N_e < 50$.

In: Wild Horses and etheir Management ...
Editor: Mathew O. Ardus, pp. 37-49

ISBN 978-1-60692-962-9

Chapter 2

AERIAL POPULATION ESTIMATES OF WILD HORSES (*EQUUS CABALLUS*) IN THE ADOBE TOWN AND SALT WELLS CREEK HERD MANAGEMENT AREAS USING AN INTEGRATED SIMULTANEOUS DOUBLE-COUNT AND SIGHTABILITY BIAS CORRECTION TECHNIQUE*

***Bruce C. Lubow*[1] *and Jason I. Ransom*[2]**
U.S. Department of the Interior, U.S. Geological Survey

ABSTRACT

An aerial survey technique combining simultaneous double-count and sightability bias correction methodologies was used to estimate the population of wild horses inhabiting Adobe Town and Salt Wells Creek Herd Management Areas, Wyoming. Based on 5 surveys over 4 years, we conclude that the technique produced estimates consistent with the known number of horses removed between surveys and an annual population growth rate of 16.2 percent per year. Therefore, evidence from this series of surveys supports the validity of this survey method. Our results also indicate that the ability of aerial observers to see horse groups is very strongly dependent on skill of the individual observer, size of the horse group, and vegetation cover. It is also more modestly dependent on the ruggedness of the terrain and the position of the sun relative to the observer. We further conclude that censuses, or uncorrected raw counts, are inadequate estimates of population size for this herd. Such uncorrected counts were all undercounts in our trials, and varied in magnitude from year to year and observer to

* This is an edited, excerpted and augmented edition of a USGS Science for a Changing World publication.

[1] Colorado State University, College of Natural Resources, Department of Fishery and Wildlife Biology, Fort Collins, Colorado 80523, USA.
[2] U.S. Geological Survey, Fort Collins Science Center, Fort Collins, Colorado 80526, USA.

observer. As of April 2007, we estimate that the population of the Adobe Town /Salt Wells Creek complex is 906 horses with a 95 percent confidence interval ranging from 857 to 981 horses.

INTRODUCTION

A census is defined as a total count, without error, of a population. Wildlife managers recognize that a census is not possible for most wildlife populations and that some estimation technique is necessary. Two factors contribute to this conclusion. First, aerial observers are unlikely to detect every individual in a population. Second, cost, personnel, and fatigue factors may make aerial surveys of vast areas prohibitive, necessitating estimation based on stratified random sampling of the area. Typically, one third or more of wild ungulates in the West (e.g., elk, mule deer, bighorn sheep, moose) are missed by uncorrected aerial counts (Samuel and others, 1987; Ackerman, 1988; Singer and Garton, 1994; Bodie and others, 1995; Bowden and Kufeld, 1995). Visibility of ungulates can vary tremendously from survey to survey depending on transect spacing and sighting factors such as snow cover, average group size, activity of the animals, tree cover, and experience of the observers (Samuel and others, 1987; Unsworth and others, 1994; Bodie and others, 1995). If sightability factors vary from survey to survey due to differences between observers and sighting conditions such as vegetation, cloud cover, snow cover, group size and others, use of one set of correction factors could be misleading. Such variability is well documented in elk. During 13 complete aerial surveys of an elk population, detection of marked elk ranged from only 41 percent under poor conditions (deep snows, small elk groups, high tree cover) to 91 percent under the best conditions (shallow, soft snow; very cold temperatures; large elk groups; large open areas) (Singer and Garton, 1994).

Two commonly used population estimation techniques are the simultaneous double-count and the sightability bias correction model. Simultaneous double-count is performed with two observers independently observing and recording data on groups of individuals, from which sighting rates are estimated by comparing the sighting records of the two observers. It is a form of mark-recapture in that animals seen by the one observer are the "marked" groups, and those that are also seen by the other observer are "resighted." Sighting probabilities for both observers can be computed from this information using Lincoln-Petersen calculations to generate a population estimate (Seber, 1973). The sightability bias correction model technique works in the opposite direction and uses a model of the sighting probability for groups of individuals, which traditionally has been precalibrated through a series of marked or ground-truthed sighting trials to determine which covariates (such as group size, percent tree and shrub cover that will hide animals, percent snow cover, observer experience, survey intensity) influence sightability. This approach was developed in Idaho for elk (Samuel and others, 1987) and thus it is often referred to as the Idaho Sightability Model.

Many traditional population estimation techniques such as simultaneous double-count and sightability bias correction models have inherent limitations, yet integrated techniques that use information from two or more such estimation methods can overcome many of the deficiencies of the individual techniques and provide greater power and efficiency (Manly and others, 1996; Borchers and others, 1998a, 1998b; Laake, 1999). For example, a major difficulty of the simultaneous double-count technique is ensuring similar sighting probabilities for all animals by each observer (Seber, 1973). This can be resolved by modeling sightability using covariates in a manner similar to the sightability bias correction technique (Samuel and others, 1987). However, unlike the traditional sightability bias correction method, multiple observers provide sufficient information to estimate sighting models for each observer from a single survey. Therefore, no precalibration of the model is required, and the often untenable assumption that the initial calibration applies uniformly over space, time, and observers is eliminated.

A stated goal of the Bureau of Land Management's (BLM) Wild Horse and Burro Program is to conduct a population survey of each herd management area at least every 4 years. However, few and infrequent surveys are inadequate for providing reliable information on which to base management decisions. Wild horse and burro managers need standardized, tested, defensible, cost- effective, yet easy-to-use aerial population estimation techniques for wild horse and burro herds in a range of habitat types and across a range of population sizes and densities. The accuracy and precision of current wild horse survey methods has not been rigorously tested; thus, a statistically valid estimation technique with confidence intervals is needed. As part of a larger research project aimed at addressing these needs (Lubow and others, 2004), we conducted a series of aerial population estimation surveys on the Adobe Town/Salt Wells Creek Herd Management Area (HMA) complex in Wyoming.

Study Area

The study area is composed of two HMAs that share a common, unobstructed border, with Adobe Town HMA on the east and Salt Wells Creek HMA on the west, as well as additional lands where horses may disperse outside of the HMA boundaries (fig. 1). The area totals 850,115 ha, with 474,555 ha lying in Salt Wells Creek HMA, 193,880 ha in Adobe Town HMA, and 181,680 ha outside of the HMAs. The complex lies in Sweetwater and Carbon Counties, Wyoming, roughly bordered on the north by US Interstate 80, on the south by the Colorado State line, on the west by US Highway 191, and on the east by Wyoming Highway 789. The area is characterized by sagebrush steppe and desert biomes with elevations ranging from 1,973 m along Sand Creek Wash to over 2,440 m on Black's Butte (U.S. Department of the Interior, 2006). Annual precipitation ranges from less than 178 mm to more than 305 mm per year and falls primarily from April through June, with the remainder falling in high-intensity summer thunderstorms and winter snowfall. Runoff from drainages is captured in reservoirs and is the primary source of water for wild horses (*Equus caballus*), livestock (*Bos* spp. and *Ovis aries)*, elk (*Cervus elaphus*), mule deer (*Odocoileus hemionus*), and pronghorn (*Antilocapra americana*). The study area is characterized by diverse plant communities that reflect wide variation in soils, topography, and geology. Predominant vegetation includes Wyoming big sagebrush (*Artemisia tridentata*), Gardner's saltbush (*Atriplex gardneri*), greasewood (*Sarcobatus vermiculatus*), bluebunch wheatgrass (*Pseudoroegneria spicata*), western wheatgrass (*Pascopyrum smithii*), and Indian ricegrass (*Oryzopsis hymenoides*). Some tree cover is present in the study area and occurs primarily in the south and west, where stands of piñon pine (*Pinus edulis*) and juniper (*Juniperus* sp.) populate the hills.

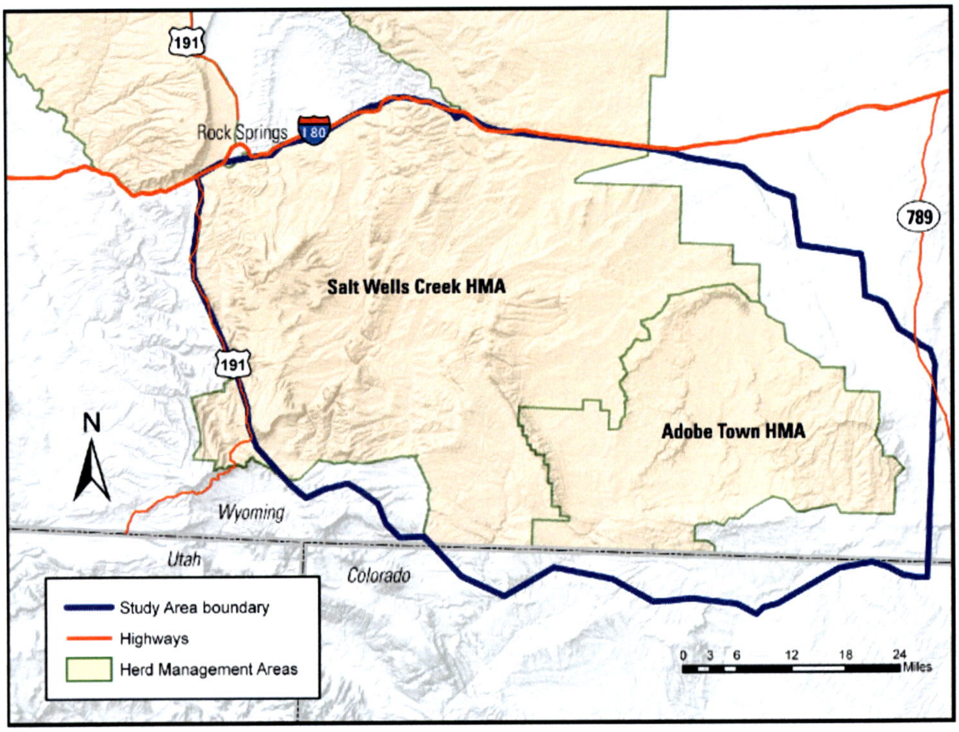

Figure 1. Location of Adobe Town and Salt Wells Creek Herd Management Areas, Wyoming, showing the boundary of the survey area.

METHODS

Aerial Surveys

To investigate an integrated aerial survey technique using the Adobe Town/Salt Wells Creek wild horse population, we performed 5 aerial surveys using a method that combined simultaneous double-count with sightability bias correction, where a known number of animals was removed between two pairs of surveys. Flights were conducted using a Cessna 210 fixed-wing aircraft, maintaining an above-ground altitude of approximately 152–183 m and airspeed of approximately 140–160 nautical miles per hour. Transects were flown north/south and spaced approximately 1.5 minutes of longitude apart (1.3 miles or 2.1 km at 41° latitude), using the same survey boundaries for each survey (fig. 2). Flight paths and group locations were recorded using a Garmin 76S Map handheld global positioning system (GPS) unit with an external antenna mounted in the front window.

The surveys were conducted on 5 occasions: (1) March 2004, (2) July 2005, (3) April 2006, (4) December 2006, and (5) April 2007. These surveys were a combined effort by BLM and USGS; survey crews were composed of individuals from both agencies, as well as an observer from the Rock Springs Grazing Association (with one exception, discussed below). The surveys contributed to the improvement of methodologies, and to testing their validity, as part of an ongoing research study. They also provided additional information for management. Surveys 2, 3, and 5 were all conducted according to the final protocols. Survey

1 was conducted differently since final protocols were not yet developed, and Survey 4 was interrupted by extreme weather. Surveys 2-5 consisted of 3 observers in addition to the pilot, whereas only 2 observers were used on Survey 1. The pilot was not considered an observer since his primary duty was flying the aircraft.

Surveys 2, 3, and 5 used the right side of the aircraft for the integrated technique by having one observer in the front seat and one observer in the rear seat directly behind him. Audio and visual isolation were maintained during the survey, with the provision that once a group of horses had passed the rear observer, the observers were free to discuss the count number and circle back if confirmation was needed. This procedure did not affect the sightability record, but ensured that the correct number of horses was recorded. The third observer, in the left rear seat, recorded the same data without being double-counted. At each fuel stop, the rear observers switched sides so that each would be double-counted during similar sighting conditions throughout the survey. Deviations from this methodology during surveys 1 and 4 are detailed below.

Survey 1 was the first survey of this population conducted under the research protocol and involving USGS personnel. Survey 1 differed substantially from subsequent 4 surveys in the following ways:

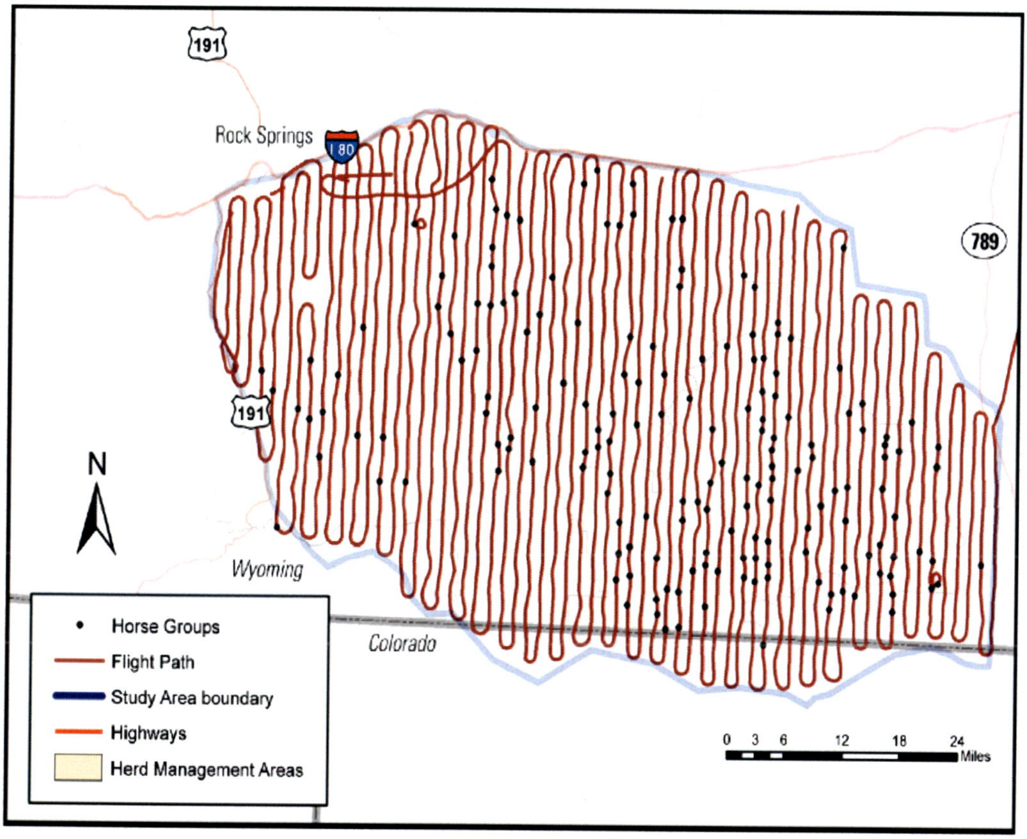

Figure 2. Flight path and locations of horse groups in the Adobe Town/Salt Wells Creek study area during the April 2007 survey. The same transect design was used for all 5 surveys.

- The survey of Adobe Town, where the majority of horses were located during Survey 1, was done with only a single rear-seat observer, who switched from one side of the airplane to the other so as to maintain a constant direction of observation as the airplane turned. All other flights were conducted with two rear observers.
- The covariates collected during the 2004 survey differed from those gathered in subsequent surveys. Specifically, vegetation cover and sun direction were not recorded in 2004. Vegetation cover has since proven to be especially important to estimating sighting probabilities.
- A different front-seat observer was used for the Salt Wells portion of the 2004 survey than was used in all subsequent surveys. Consequently, data available to estimate this observer's sighting ability are minimal.
- The 2004 survey covered only the area within the HMA boundaries; areas outside those boundaries were not searched for horses that had strayed onto adjacent non-BLM land. This deficiency was corrected in later surveys.
- The dual-observer technique was new to all but one crewmember on this first flight; therefore, inexperience may have affected the results.

Survey 4, in December 2006, was interrupted by weather. The full survey methodology was used over 3 days before bad weather interrupted the survey for several days. Following the interruption, a second phase of the survey covered most of the remaining area and resulted in 333 additional horse observations. However, this second phase was not included in the research study because timing caused by weather delays prevented USGS involvement in this portion of the survey. As a result, the simultaneous double-count methodology was not used and covariates were not recorded.

Data Analysis

Program MARK (White and Burnham, 1999; White and others, 2001) was used to model the simultaneous double-count data. The Huggins closed-capture model structure (Huggins, 1989; 1991) implemented in program MARK was chosen because it enables use of covariates. This method uses a conditional likelihood approach to model the probability of sighting each horse group based on the covariates recorded for that group. We considered covariates for survey occasion, observer, seat location (front or rear), group size, distance from aircraft, rugged versus flat terrain, type of vegetation cover, percent vegetation cover, percent snow cover, sun position, and movement of the horses. In addition, the interactions of group size with open vegetation and group size with rugged terrain were considered.

Separate sightability models were fitted for Survey 1 versus the remaining 4 surveys combined, because the methods used and data collected for Survey 1 were incompatible with the other 4. The latter model of sighting probabilities (based on Surveys 2-5) was able to draw on this much larger dataset to obtain the most precise possible estimates, but individual population estimates were made for each survey.

To handle Survey 4's two phases and their different methods, we used only the results of the first phase in our modeling and analysis to determine sighting probabilities for each horse group individually. We then used the average sighting probability for that entire phase to correct the additional raw count from the second phase and added these two components together to reach a final estimate. We also assumed that the error rate (coefficient of variation) for the second phase was 30 percent, because the data collected provide no means to estimate the precision statistically. We chose this high error rate to allow for the differences in observers and methods and for any other unknown errors.

Horses were assumed to be available to either the two right-side observers or to the single left-side observer and never available to both. Groups seen only by the pilot were dropped from the analysis because pilot survey effort was highly variable. Rear-seat observers were rotated so that each could be tested against the front-seat observer, enabling estimation of unique sighting probability models for each observer.

Approximately 6.8 percent of the survey area fell within a 1 37-m strip underneath the airplane's flight path that was not visible to the observers while flying directly overhead. However, in this analysis, we did not increase our estimates to account for horses that might have been missed within this area. This is justified by assuming that horses located in this strip might run from the approaching aircraft and become visible, or that they could be spotted from an adjacent transect with some probability. This assumption also minimizes the possibility of an overestimate. We also found that the population model discussed below fit better without an adjustment for horses missed under the flight path.

Final population estimates were computed using AICc model weights (Burnham and Anderson, 2002) to weight the complete set of tested models. This process accounts for the inherent uncertainty in the selection of the model from the candidate set, thereby widening the confidence intervals to realistically reflect this often-overlooked source of uncertainty. Population estimates were computed using the sighting probabilities for each individual group to correct for groups not seen (Huggins, 1989, 1991). The observed group sizes were applied to the corrected group number and summed to obtain the population estimate.

A bootstrap procedure was used to compute confidence intervals for the population estimates (Wong, 1996). Alternative sighting models were fit to the bootstrapped data; thus, variation in estimates includes that caused by sightability model selection, model parameter estimation, and the binomial sighting process itself. Confidence intervals were computed assuming lognormal errors.

Population Modeling

A simple population model was constructed to project the population from one time period to the next. The population increase from 1 year to the next was projected as a constant percentage of the previous population. This combines births and deaths, which is necessary because no data on these separate processes are available for this population. A removal of 1,200 horses occurred in September 2005, and another 846 horses were removed in January 2007. A much larger removal of 2,350 horses occurred in August 2003, before the first survey in this study. These known removals were subtracted from the population projections. Thus, the model required only two parameters to be estimated: the initial population size and the annual population growth rate (net of births and deaths).

The population model was fit to the field estimates of population size following the methods of White and Lubow (2002). Optimum model fit was determined by finding the parameter values that minimized the squared differences between model values and field estimates, weighted by the precision of the field estimates. The estimate from Survey 1 was excluded in the fitting due to the different methodology employed in that entire survey; however, the estimates from Survey 4 were included, despite the noted differences in methodology for a portion of this survey.

RESULTS

Of 15 models examined, the model most strongly supported by the complete dataset (Surveys 2–5) included separate intercept parameters for each observer and common slope parameters across observers for the effects of group size, presence of vegetation, terrain, and relative sun position. Sighting probability differed markedly among observers and was very strongly dependent on group size (fig. 3). Estimated sighting probability for a single horse varied from as low as 13.2 percent to as high as 65.5 percent, depending on the observer and sighting conditions. Sighting probability increased sharply with group size; essentially all groups larger than 20 horses were seen. Presence of vegetation, rugged terrain, and looking toward the sun on a clear day all reduced sighting probability compared to the opposite conditions.

The most general model (most parameters) fit the data very well and showed no evidence of over-dispersion. The variance inflation factor was 1.0, exactly the expected value for a binomial process with full independence. Alternative models with sufficient support to be considered differed in the presence or absence of the rugged terrain covariate, the inclusion of a sun elevation- angle covariate, and additive effects of the survey date (i.e., a general increase or decrease in sighting probability for an entire survey). The best model received 35.6 percent of the weight and only the top 5 received >5 percent each. The population estimates were based on weighted-average estimates from these top 5 models.

Actual numbers of horses seen along with the statistical estimates are provided in table 1. Average sighting rates for entire surveys ranged between 70.2 percent and 84.2 percent. Across the 4 most recent surveys, average sighting probability was 77.1 percent. Estimated error rates (coefficient of variation) for population estimates ranged from 3.1 percent to 8.1 percent across the surveys.

There was a single pair of surveys conducted before and after known gather and removal operations without an intervening period of births. The removal of 846 horses in January 2007 is significantly smaller ($P< 0.0$ 16) than the difference in our December 2006 and April 2007 estimates. The estimated change is 1,180 [909 – 1,451]. The actual change does not fall within the 95 percent confidence interval.

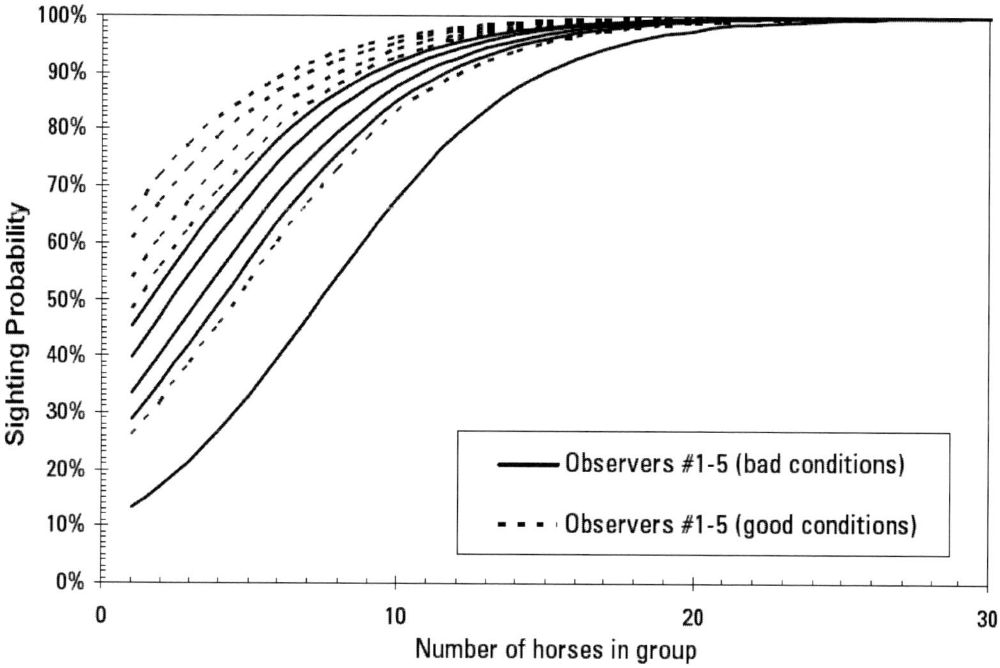

Figure 3. Sighting probabilities by horse group size and observer. Good conditions (dashed lines) correspond to no obscuring vegetation (shrubs or trees), non-rugged terrain, and sun not shining toward observer. Bad conditions (solid lines) are the reverse. The set of 5 lines of each type represent sighting models for the 5 different observers who participated in the surveys.

The model estimate for December 2006 is near the lower 95 percent confidence bound for that estimate despite the estimate having a larger confidence interval than the others. The low precision is due to the assumed (rather than statistically estimated) low precision for the second phase of the survey, which was not conducted using the research methodology.

We currently estimate 906 [857–981] horses in this population. If the lower confidence interval bound of the current estimate is assumed and the 16.2 percent growth rate is applied, the projected population later in 2007 will be at least 996 horses.

Table 1. Combined population estimates for the Adobe Town and Salt Wells Creek Herd Management Areas

Survey date	Horses seen (No.)	Population estimate (No.)	Population seen (%)	SE	CV (%)	LCL (95%)	UCL (95%)
Mar-04[1]	1,253	1,536	81.6	75.0	4.9	1,423	1,725
Jul-05	1,552	2,211	70.2	113.5	5.1	2,023	2,473
Apr-06	1,189	1,541	77.2	47.5	3.1	1,460	1,647
Dec-06[2]	1,385	2,088	82.3	170.1	8.1	1,875	2,591
Apr-07	763	906	84.2	31.1	3.4	857	981

[1] Estimate made using different survey methods and different analysis methods.

[2] The December 2006 estimate is based on two phases of the survey, only one of which used the same methods as other surveys.

Discussion

The fitted population model places the five individual estimates into a comprehensive picture. In fitting the population model, all the individual estimates are integrated and combined with simple population dynamics to find a trajectory for this population consistent with all of the available information. The fitted population model falls within the 95 percent confidence intervals of the field population estimates for all estimates except that in 2004 (which was excluded in the model fitting due to differences in methods used for this early estimate). The model growth rate that provides the best fit is 16.2 percent, which is certainly plausible based on observed annual growth rates in other herds, which range from 15 percent to 25 percent per year (Eberhardt and others 1982; Garrott and Taylor, 1990; Garrott and others, 1991). This provides some confirmation that the individual estimates are valid, because they all can be plausibly linked to each other through known removals and a realistic estimate of population growth rate.

Given the population growth rate estimated in this analysis and the large removal that occurred just prior to the first survey, it is possible to project backwards in time to estimate the maximum population size reached prior to this series of removals. This calculation estimates that 4,370 horses were present in 2003, after the birth of young and before the removal later that summer.

In light of all of the subsequent evidence, the 2004 population estimate (Survey 1) was considerably biased (low). The fitted population model suggests that the population in 2004 should have been 2020 horses, which is 484 horses more than our estimate at the time. Thus, it appears that the estimate was low by 24 percent. The numerous differences in methodology, which have since been improved, are undoubtedly the reason that this first estimate was so low.

Although the population model fits within the 95 percent confidence intervals of the December 2006 field estimate, it is close to the lower bound, suggesting that this field estimate may be too high. The most plausible reason for this is that the second phase of the survey was conducted several days after the end of the first phase because of weather conditions. It is possible that horses moved during the intervening period and that some were erroneously counted twice (during both phases). The difference in methods applied during the second phase may also have contributed unknown errors to this estimate.

The fitted population model (fig. 4) produced a population growth rate estimate of 16.2 percent/year. The population model estimates are all within the 95 percent confidence intervals of the field estimates, excluding the March 2004 estimate, which was not included in the model fitting. This estimate from Survey 1 is clearly an outlier, 24 percent lower than the fitted population model projects that it should have been.

The problem with the December 2006 estimate also impacts the comparison of the population before and after the known removal in January 2007. The estimated population reduction is larger than the actual known removal. However, the above explanation for the apparent overestimate in December 2006 also explains the overestimate of this reduction. In addition, it is possible that some mortality, especially of young, occurred during the 4-month period between the surveys, adding to the known population reduction caused by the removal operation. Any such natural mortality would bring the actual and estimated reduction values closer to agreement.

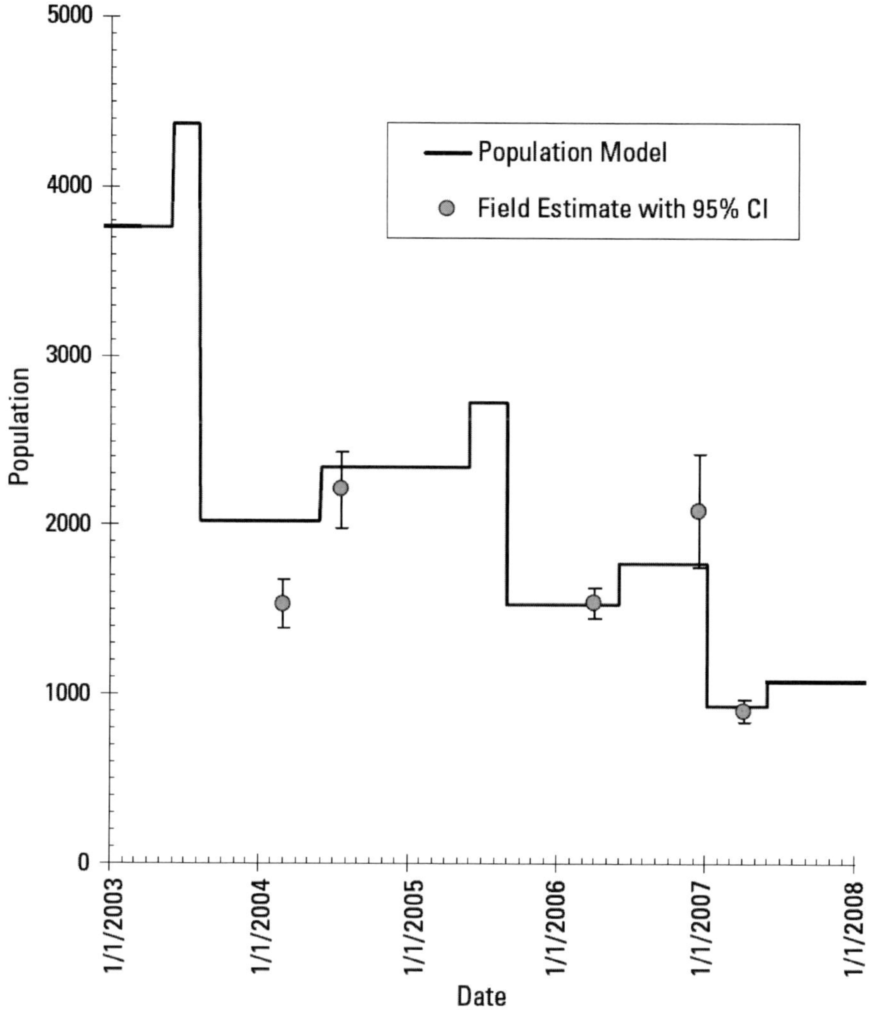

Figure 4. Population projection model fitted to observed field estimates of population size, shown with 95 percent confidence intervals. The field estimate in 2004 was excluded from the model fitting because of substantial differences in methodology between that one and the remaining four estimates. Increasing population segments represent estimated new recruitment of young net of any natural mortality; decreasing segments represent known management removals. An annual population growth rate of 16.2 percent was estimated to produce the best fit to the data.

Conclusion

The double-count method for correcting visibility bias is theoretically biased to produce underestimates of true population size. This bias arises from the fact that not all horse groups are equally visible. The addition of sighting covariates to model differences in sighting probability among groups partially corrects for this bias, but unless these models are nearly perfect, undercounting is still possible. The results of this analysis, however, provide no indication that a negative bias is present. First, there is no indication of over-dispersion in the data. Over-dispersion is an expected consequence of non-independent observations. Second, the population model fits the estimates in light of the known removals quite well, which would not be the case if the population estimates were seriously biased. However, if some small bias remains, it would cause the population size to be underestimated, leading managers to remove fewer horses than they should, providing a conservative safety margin against removing too many animals.

Our results indicate that the ability of aerial observers to see horse groups is very strongly dependent on skill of the individual observer, size of the horse group, and vegetation cover. It is also more modestly dependent on the ruggedness of the terrain and the position of the sun. There is also some evidence that sighting conditions vary from one survey to the next. Finally, 100 percent sighting probability is only achieved for a few large horse groups. Thus, raw counts will almost always underestimate true population.

In conclusion, the integrated simultaneous double-count/sightability bias correction technique provided considerably more valid aerial population estimation results than the standard uncorrected aerial census method, and disclosed important variables that can affect the outcome of an aerial survey in this study area. The results were validated by known removals and realistic population growth rates, providing further support for the integrated technique and a better understanding of methodology for improving future aerial surveys of the Adobe Town and Salt Wells Creek Herd Management Areas.

REFERENCES

Ackerman, B.B., 1988, *Visibility bias of mule deer aerial census procedures in southwest Idaho:* Moscow, University of Idaho, Ph.D. dissertation, 106 p.

Bodie, W.L., Garton, E.O., Taylor, E.R., and McCoy, M., 1995, A sightability model for bighorn sheep in canyon habitats: *Journal of Wildlife Management,* v. 59, p. 832–840.

Borchers, D.L., Buckland, S.T., Goedhart, P.W., Clarke, E.D., and Hedley, S.L., 1998a, Horvitz-Thompson estimators for double-platform line-transect surveys: Biometrics, v. 54, p. 1221–1237. Borchers, D.L., Zucchini, W., and Fewster, R.M., 1998b, Mark-recapture models for line-transect surveys: *Biometrics,* v. 54, p. 1207–1220.

Bowden, D.L. and Kufeld, R.C., 1995, Generalized mark-resight population size estimation applied to Colorado moose: *Journal of Wildlife Management,* v. 59, p. 840–851.

Burnham, K.P., and Anderson, D.R., 2002, *Model selection and multimodel inference—a practical information-theoretic approach* (2nd ed.): New York, Springer-Verlag, 488 p.

Eberhardt, L.L., Majorowicz, A.K., and Wilcox, J.A., 1982, Apparent rates of increase for two feral horse herds: *Journal of Wildlife Management,* v. 46, p. 367–374.

Garrott, R.A., Siniff, D.B., and Eberhardt, L.L., 1991, Growth rates of feral horse populations: *Journal of Wildlife Management,* v. 55, p. 641–648.

Garrott, R.A., and Taylor, L., 1990, Dynamics of a feral horse population in Montana: *Journal of Wildlife Management,* v. 54, p. 603–612.

Huggins, R.M., 1989, *On the statistical analysis of capture-recapture experiments: Biometrika,* v. 76, p. 133–140.

Huggins, R.M., 1991, Some practical aspects of a conditional likelihood approach to capture experiments: *Biometrics,* v. 47, p. 725–732.

Laake, J.L., 1999, Distance sampling with independent observers—reducing bias from heterogeneity by weakening the conditional independence assumption, *in* Garner, G.W., Amstrup, S.C., Laake, J.L., Manly, B.F.J., McDonald, L.L., and Robertson, D.G., eds., *Marine mammal survey and assessment methods:* Rotterdam, Netherlands, A.A. Balkema, p. 137–148.

Lubow, B., Ransom, J.I., and Singer, F.J., 2004, Aerial population estimation for wild horses and burros—work plan: *U.S. Geological Survey, Biological Resources Discipline, and Colorado State University*, Fort Collins, Colo., 25 p.

Manly, B.F.J., McDonald, L., and Garner, G.W., 1996, Maximum likelihood estimation for the double-count method with independent observers: *Journal of Biological and Environmental Statistics,* v. 1, p. 170–189.

Samuel, M.D., Garton, E.O., Schlegal, M.W., and Carson, R.G., 1987, Visibility bias during aerial surveys of elk in northcentral Idaho: *Journal of Wildlife Management,* v. 51, p. 622–630.

Seber, G.A.F., 1973, *The estimation of animal abundance and related parameters*: New York, Hafner Press, 506 p.

Singer, F.J., and Garton, E., 1994, Elk sightability model for the Super Cub, *in* Unsworth, J.W., Leban, F.A., Leptich, D.J., Garton, E., and Zager, P., *Aerial survey—user's manual* (2nd ed.): Boise, Idaho Department of Fish and Game, p. 47–49.

Unsworth, J.W., Leban, F.A., Leptich, D.J., Garton, E., and Zager, P., 1994, *Aerial survey—user's manual* (2nd ed.): Boise, Idaho Department of Fish and Game, 84 p.

U.S. Department of the Interior, 2006, *Adobe Town–Salt Wells Creek Herd Management Area Complex Population Management Action and Environmental Assessment,* WY040-07-EA-37: Rock Springs and Rawlins Field Offices, Wyoming, Bureau of Land Management, 44 p.

White, G.C., and Burnham, K.P., 1999, *Program MARK—survival estimation from populations of marked animals: Bird Study* 46 (Supplement), p. 120–138.

White, G.C., Burnham, K.P., and Anderson, D.R., 2001, Advanced features of Program MARK, *in* Field, R., Warren, R.J., Okarma, H., and Sievert, P.R., eds., Wildlife, land, and people—priorities for the 21st Century: Bethesda, Md., *Proceedings of the Second International Wildlife Management Congress,* The Wildlife Society, p. 368–377.

White, G.C., and Lubow, B.C., 2002, Fitting population models to multiple sources of observed data: *Journal of Wildlife Management,* v. 66, p. 300–309.

Wong, C.N., 1996, Population size estimation using the modified Horvitz-Thompson Estimator with estimated sighting probability: Fort Collins, Colorado State University, *Ph.D. dissertation,* 202 p.

In: Wild Horses and etheir Management ... ISBN 978-1-60692-962-9
Editor: Mathew O. Ardus, pp. 51-112

Chapter 3

BUREAU OF LAND MANAGEMENT: EFFECTIVE LONG-TERM OPTIONS NEEDED TO MANAGE UNADOPTABLE WILD HORSES*

United States Government Accountability Office

WHAT GAO FOUND

BLM has made significant progress toward setting and meeting AML (the optimum number of animals which results in a thriving natural ecological balance and avoids range deterioration). BLM has set AML for 197 out of 199 HMAs. Most of the field offices GAO surveyed considered similar factors in determining AML, such as rangeland conditions; however, BLM has not provided specific formal guidance to the field offices on how to set AML. Without clear guidance, BLM cannot ensure that the factors considered in future AML revisions will be consistent across HMAs. At a national level, in 2007, BLM was closer to meeting AML (about 27,200 animals) than in any other year since AMLs were first reported in 1984. The extent to which BLM has actually met AML depends on the accuracy of BLM's population counts. Nineteen of the 26 field officials GAO surveyed used a counting method which, researchers say, consistently undercounts animals and does not provide a statistical range of population estimates. Undercounting can put animals at risk and lead to increased program costs.

The number of animals removed from the range is far greater than the number adopted or sold, which has resulted in the need for increased short-term and long-term holding. Since 2001, over 74,000 animals have been removed from the range, while only about 46,400 have been adopted or sold. Thirty-six percent fewer animals were adopted in 2007 than compared to the average adoption rates in the 1990s. As of June 2008, BLM was holding 30,088

* This is an edited, excerpted and augmented edition of a United States Government Accountability Office publication, No.: GAO-09-77, dated October 2008.

animals in holding facilities, up from 9,807 in 2001. To accommodate the increased removals and declining adoptions and sales, BLM has increased the number of short-term and long-term holding facilities.

BLM has implemented multiple controls to help ensure humane treatment, including random checks on adopted horses and agreements with adopters and buyers to prevent slaughter. Although BLM state offices collect data on the treatment of the animals, BLM does not always compile the information in its central database or report it to the public. Providing additional information to the public on the treatment of these animals could help inform the public about their treatment and improve transparency.

The long-term sustainability of BLM's Wild Horse and Burro Program depends on the resolution of two significant challenges:

If not controlled, off-the-range holding costs will continue to overwhelm the program. The percentage of the program's direct costs for holding animals off the range increased from $7 million in 2000 (46 percent) to $21 million in 2007 (67 percent). In 2008, these costs could account for 74 percent of the program's budget.

BLM has limited options for dealing with unadoptable animals. The act provides that unadopted excess animals shall be humanely destroyed or, under certain circumstances, sold without limitation. However, BLM only manages these animals through sales with limitations. BLM is concerned about the possible reaction to the destruction of healthy animals.

Why GAO Did this Study

The Department of the Interior's Bureau of Land Management (BLM) manages about 33,100 wild horses and burros on 199 Herd Management Areas (HMA) in

10 western states. Under the Wild Free-Roaming Horses and Burros Act of 1971, as amended, BLM is to protect wild horses and burros, set appropriate management levels (AML), maintain current inventory counts, and remove excess animals to prevent overpopulation and rangeland damage. Over the years, various stakeholders have raised issues about BLM's management of the animals on and off the range.

GAO examined (1) BLM's progress in setting and meeting AML; BLM's management of animals off the range through adoptions, sales, and holding facilities; BLM's controls to help ensure the humane treatment of animals; and (4) what challenges, if any, BLM faces in managing for the long-term sustainability of the program. GAO surveyed and analyzed documents from 26 of the 44 BLM offices that manage wild horses and burros

What GAO Recommends

To improve the program, GAO is recommending, among other things, that BLM establish a formal policy for setting AML, develop alternatives for long-term holding facilities, and initiate a discussion with Congress and other stakeholders on how best to comply with the act, as amended. The Department of the Interior concurred with GAO's findings and recommendations.

ABBREVIATIONS

AML	appropriate management level
BLM	Bureau of Land Management
HMA	Herd Management Area

October 9, 2008
The Honorable Nick J. Rahall, II Chairman
Committee on Natural Resources House of Representatives

Dear Mr. Chairman:

Wild horses have long been a symbol of the independence of the American West, but today, the health of their population depends heavily on government management. At their peak, in the mid-1800s, an estimated 2 million wild horses roamed America's rangelands. Populations decreased as development reduced habitat for wild horses and native grazers and as horses and burros were rounded up to make room for livestock and farming operations. By the early 1900s, most wild horses had disappeared from the Great Plains and those that remained were found primarily in the remote mountains, deserts, and badlands of the West. By 1971, only about 9,500 wild horses were thought to live on public rangelands. Public concerns about abuse and wild horse population declines swelled in the 1950s and 1960s. Subsequently, Congress enacted the Wild Free-Roaming Horses and Burros Act of 1971 to protect wild horses and burros from abuse and death and to manage them to achieve and maintain a thriving natural ecological balance on the public lands.[1] The 1971 act declared these wild animals to be "living symbols of the historic and pioneer spirit of the West; that they contribute to the diversity of life forms within the Nation and enrich the lives of the American people; and that these horses and burros are fast disappearing from the American scene." Since the passage of the act, wild horse and burro populations have increased, but the way they are managed on public lands has been controversial and wild horse advocates continue to voice concerns about horses being slaughtered.

The 1971 act authorized and directed the Secretary of the Interior, on public lands managed by the Bureau of Land Management (BLM), and the Secretary of Agriculture, on public lands managed by the Forest Service, "to protect and manage wild free-roaming horses and burros as components of public lands."[2] The act also directed the Secretaries to manage them "to achieve and maintain a thriving natural ecological balance on the public lands." BLM field offices are responsible for determining where the animals are to be managed within areas where they were found as of 1971.[3] In fiscal year 2007, the program was funded at $36.4 million under BLM's Management of Lands and Resources appropriation. Forty-four BLM field units manage approximately 33,100 wild horses and burros on 199 Herd Management Areas (HMA) covering over 34 million acres in 10 western states—Arizona, California, Colorado, Idaho, Montana, New Mexico, Nevada, Oregon, Utah, and Wyoming.[4] BLM's Nevada State Office manages about half of the land and animals in the Wild Horse and Burro Program.

In the mid- to late 1970s, population counts indicated that there was a large increase in wild horses and burros and that they were contributing to overgrazing of the rangeland. Congress amended the 1971 act in 1978 to protect the range from wild horse overpopulation, among other things.

The Public Rangelands Improvement Act of 1978 directed the Secretaries of the Interior and Agriculture to determine appropriate management levels (AML), maintain a current inventory of wild horses and burros, and determine whether and where overpopulation exists.[5] AML has been defined as the "optimum number of wild horses which results in a thriving natural ecological balance and avoids deterioration of the range."[6] Each BLM field office is responsible for determining AML for each of the HMAs it manages. The aggregate AML for BLM's 199 HMAs is approximately 27,200. Because wild horse populations can double every 4 years and few natural predators remain, managing wild horse and burro populations at AML has become a primary objective of the program. To reach and maintain AML, BLM primarily conducts "gathers" to remove excess animals from the range. From 1971 through 2007, over 267,000 wild horses and burros were removed.[7] In 2001, BLM began implementing its most recent management strategy, to reach AML by increasing removals. Since then, about 10,600 animals have been removed, on average, per year.

Maintaining current and accurate inventories of wild horses and burros is a key component of on-the-range management. BLM has traditionally counted animals using the direct-count method, which involves flying over the HMA and reporting on each individual animal they see. BLM generally conducts this type of animal count or "census" every 4 years or so, leading up to a removal of excess animals. To produce annual population estimates between counts, BLM adjusts these census figures for each HMA based on an estimate of the herd's annual population growth. If the census numbers are inaccurate, particularly if they underestimate the actual population, BLM runs the risk that adequate forage or water may not be available for the wild horses and burros or for livestock and wildlife in the area.

After being removed from the range, excess animals are managed in short- term holding facilities, where they are either prepared for adoption or sale, or in long-term holding facilities, where they will live out the remainder of their lives. The preferred outcome for healthy animals removed from the range is that they be adopted through BLM's Adopt-a-Horse-or-Burro Program. As of 2007, approximately 235,700 animals have been adopted by the public since the start of the program in 1971. On average, about 6,300 wild horses and burros have been adopted annually since 2001. Under the act, as amended, BLM is required to assure that adopters can provide humane treatment and care.[8] When adoption demand is not sufficient to absorb all the animals removed, the act, as amended, directs BLM to either destroy the remaining healthy animals in the most humane and cost-efficient manner possible or, under certain circumstances, sell them without limitation.[9] BLM has not destroyed any animals since January 1982, when a former BLM director issued a moratorium to end the destruction of excess unadoptable animals. To manage for the growing number of unadoptable animals, BLM began opening long-term holding facilities. Unlike the rangelands of the West where the animals normally live, the long-term holding facilities use Midwest grasslands that generally provide the animals with abundant forage and decreased stress. This allows most of the animals to live far longer than they would in the wild. BLM pays the private contractors that operate the long-term holding facilities a fee per horse per day. The sales directive, which was enacted on December 8, 2004, directs BLM to sell excess wild horses and burros without limitation if the animal is more than 10 years of age or has been offered unsuccessfully for adoption at least three times.[10]

Since the passage of the 1971 act, there has been controversy over the number of wild horses and burros that BLM manages in the wild and the amount of public land available for their management. There is concern by some, including wild horse and burro advocacy groups, that the number of animals managed in the wild is too low to protect their genetic integrity; that the numbers are based on insufficient rangeland monitoring data; and that BLM gives preference to other users of the range, primarily livestock and wildlife. For instance, groups often point out that BLM permits far more cattle and sheep to graze on BLM managed lands than horses. Specifically, in fiscal year 2007, approximately 567,000 head of cattle or sheep grazed BLM public lands.[11] However, livestock are managed on 160 million acres of BLM lands, compared to the 29 million BLM acres that are available for wild horses and burros.[12] Additionally, advocacy groups are concerned that the animals removed from the range are too often adopted into abusive homes or are ultimately sold for slaughter. Some livestock and wildlife groups argue that the population of wild horses and burros has far exceeded the level that provides ecological balance and equitable forage distribution for competing users, such as cattle and sage grouse.

We first reviewed BLM's Wild Horse and Burro Program in 1990.[13] At that time, regarding on-the-range management activities, we found that BLM's decisions on how many wild horses to remove from federal rangelands were not based on direct evidence that wild horse populations exceeded what the range could support and that removals were often not accompanied by reductions in livestock grazing levels or range management to increase the land's capacity. We recommended that BLM develop carrying capacity and range condition data and, in locations where overgrazing was occurring, that BLM implement range management techniques designed to give vegetation more opportunity to grow and, when necessary, remove wild horses and reduce livestock grazing in proportion to the numbers of each species on the range. Regarding off-therange management activities, we found that "BLM's wild horse sanctuaries [long-term holding facilities] are likely to be much more expensive than originally envisioned and may represent only a temporary solution to the disposal of unadoptable horses.... If horse removals above levels that can be handled by private adoptions are reinstituted, other disposal options will have to be considered." We recommended that BLM consider a variety of disposal options for unadoptable horses and, as necessary, make recommendations for congressional consideration.

To update our 1990 report, we are reporting on (1) BLM's progress in managing wild horses and burros on the range through setting and meeting AML; (2) BLM's management of wild horses and burros off of the range through adoption, sales, and holding facilities; (3) the controls BLM has in place to help ensure humane treatment of wild horses and burros; and (4) what challenges, if any, BLM faces in managing the long-term sustainability of the Wild Horse and Burro Program. We were also asked to review how and why the acreage available for wild horses and burros had changed since the 1971 act. We did not examine the acreage issue because BLM is in the process of compiling a history of acreage determinations. BLM officials expect their review to be completed by March 2009.

To examine how BLM manages wild horses and burros on and off of the range and to identify the challenges facing BLM, we reviewed relevant laws, regulations, BLM policies, and strategic plans. We also surveyed, and analyzed documents from, 26 of the 44 BLM field offices that manage wild horses and burros.[14] We collected and reviewed relevant resource management decision documents from the surveyed field offices to help corroborate their responses about specific questions, including those about factors used to make AML determinations and gather decisions. In addition, we also conducted follow-up phone calls to clarify ambiguous or incomplete survey responses. We received usable responses from all field offices that we surveyed—a 100 percent response rate. We surveyed field offices in all 10 western states that have HMAs. The field offices we surveyed represented 82 percent of all BLM acres managed for wild horses and burros, 74 percent of all BLM managed wild horses, and 69 percent of burros on the range at the time of our survey. We interviewed BLM Wild Horse and Burro Program managers at the state and national levels and conducted site visits at two field offices that manage HMAs, two adoption events, three short-term holding facilities, and one long-term holding facility. To examine humane treatment, we collected information from BLM's compliance database and interviewed public citizens, advocacy groups, and BLM officials. A more detailed description of our scope and methodology is presented in appendix I.

We conducted this performance audit from September 2007 to October 2008 in accordance with generally accepted government auditing standards. Those standards require that we plan and perform the audit to obtain sufficient, appropriate evidence to provide a reasonable basis for our findings and conclusions based on our audit objectives. We believe that the evidence obtained provides a reasonable basis for our findings and conclusions based on our audit objectives.

Results in Brief

BLM has made significant progress in setting and meeting AML for the HMAs. As of February 2008, BLM has set AML for 197 out of 199 HMAs. Most of the field offices we surveyed considered similar factors in determining AML, such as rangeland conditions and climate data; however, BLM has not provided specific formal guidance to the field offices on how to set AML. BLM has been working on revising the program's handbook to provide this guidance since 2006. Without clear guidance, BLM cannot ensure that the factors considered in future AML revisions will be consistent across HMAs, especially since the personnel most familiar with the current, informal practice of determining AML are retiring at an increasing rate. At the national level, BLM was closer to meeting AML in 2007 than in any other year since AMLs were first reported in 1984. Specifically, in February 2007, BLM estimated the population of wild horses and burros to be 28,563, about 1,000 animals over AML. To reach this level, BLM has reduced the nationwide population in the wild by about 40 percent since 2000. Our 1990 report was critical of BLM's decisions on the number of wild horses and burros to remove from the range. At that time we concluded that the decisions were made without adequate information about range carrying capacity or the impact of the animals on range conditions. Since then, in August 2005, BLM updated its formal policy on gathers and removals and specified the key factors that should be considered in the decision making process. The extent to which BLM has actually met AML depends on the accuracy of its population counts. Nineteen of the 26 field officials we surveyed used the direct-count method for their most recent gathers. This method, according to researchers, consistently undercounts animals and does not provide a statistical range of population estimates. Some

BLM officials are concerned that other counting methods would require too much additional staff or are too expensive. However, undercounting is also costly since it often leads BLM to remove fewer animals than needed, which leads to overpopulation and costlier gathers in the future. For example, in the summer of 2007, BLM staff on an HMA in Nevada miscalculated the population by approximately 640 wild horses and found that the actual population was about five times greater than what they determined was sustainable. Many of the wild horses subsequently removed from this HMA were in poor condition due to severe drought, and about 150 animals ultimately died from disease in short-term holding as a result.

The number of wild horses and burros removed from the range is far greater than the number adopted or sold, which has resulted in a significant increase in the number of animals in short- and long-term holding and commensurate increases in spending for their care. Since 2001, over 74,000 animals have been removed from the range, while only about 46,400 have been adopted or sold. Thirty-six percent fewer wild horses and burros were adopted in 2007, compared to average adoption rates in the 1990s. BLM officials attribute the steady adoption decline in recent years to the decreasing demand for horses in general and increasing hay and fuel costs associated with their care. As of June 2008, BLM was holding 30,088 animals in short- and long-term holding facilities, far more than in 2001 when it held 9,807. From 2001 through June 2008, the number of short-term holding facilities increased from 14 to 24 to accommodate more animals, while the average cost per animal increased from $3.00 per day to $5.08 per day. The total cost for short-term holding increased from $6.4 million in 2000 to $11.2 million in 2001. From 2001 through 2007, the cost remained relatively stable, but for 2008, costs are anticipated to increase to $16.2 million. Similarly, BLM has increased the number of longterm holding facilities from 1 in 1988 to 11 as of June 2008, and the average cost per animal has increased to approximately $1.27 per day. Warnings issued in the 1990s by us and the Department of the Interior's Office of Inspector General about the potential for escalating costs for long-term holding have proven accurate, as spending on long-term holding has increased from about $668,000 in 2000 to more than $9.1 million in 2007. In addition, with the long-term holding facilities at full capacity—they held 22,101 wild horses as of June 2008 and had a capacity of 22,100—more wild horses are spending a longer time in the more expensive short-term holding facilities.

BLM has implemented multiple controls to help ensure the humane treatment of wild horses and burros, including standard operating procedures, random checks on adopted horses, and agreements with buyers to help prevent slaughter. For gathers, it has established standard operating procedures and reporting systems to help ensure humane treatment. According to data from 6 of the 10 states that manage wild horses and burros, 1.2 percent of animals removed from 2005 to 2007 were either euthanized or died accidentally. While BLM state offices sometimes collect data on animals that die during gathers, the information is not compiled by BLM headquarters in its centralized database, nor is it reported to the public. For animals held after removal in short- and longterm holding facilities, staff from BLM and veterinarians from the Department of Agriculture's Animal and Plant Health Inspection Service inspect facilities on a regular basis to help ensure adequate care and treatment are provided. For wild horses and burros that have been adopted, BLM guidance directs field offices to make follow-up phone calls or visits for all adopters during the first year of the adoption, physically inspect a random sample of adopted animals, and conduct inspections of adopted animals whenever complaints are received. According to the results of BLM's random adoption inspections, from 2005 through 2007, on average about 9 percent of adopters did not comply with BLM standards of care for adopted wild horses and burros. The most common violations were failing to report changes in the animals' status or location to BLM and failing to provide adequate facilities or care. For animals that are sold, since the spring of 2005, BLM has required buyers to sign a statement that they do not intend to slaughter the animals. Although BLM tracks information about the treatment of animals in short- and long-term holding and after adoption, it does not regularly report this information to the public. Doing so could help inform the public about the treatment of the animals and improve transparency.

The long-term sustainability of BLM's Wild Horse and Burro Program depends on the resolution of two significant challenges:

- *If not controlled, off-the-range holding costs will continue to overwhelm the program.* The Wild Horse and Burro Program's spending for off-the-range holding increased from $7 million in 2000— 46 percent of the program's direct costs—to about $21 million in 2007—67 percent of the program's direct costs. In 2008, BLM anticipates that holding costs will account for about 74 percent of the program's direct costs. As holding costs continue to increase, less funding is available for on-the-range management, which could result in sharp increases to the animal population in the wild. To deal with its long-term holding problem, BLM has primarily sought increased funding to open additional holding facilities. However, funding is not likely to increase in the future, and limited funding is forcing BLM to make the difficult choice among managing the animals on the range to prevent overpopulation, destroying excess unadoptable animals, or selling them without limitation. If funding is not increased or if BLM does not dispose of animals in other ways, BLM projects that the number of wild horses on the range would reach about 50,000, or about 80 percent over AML, by 2012.
- *BLM's options are limited for dealing with unadoptable animals.* The Wild Free-Roaming Horses and Burros Act, as amended, requires that excess animals, for which the adoption demand is not sufficient to absorb all the animals removed from the range, be destroyed in the most humane and cost-efficient manner possible or, under certain circumstances, be sold without limitation. From fiscal year 1988 through fiscal year 2004, Congress prohibited BLM from using its Management of Lands and Resources appropriations to destroy excess healthy, unadopted wild horses and burros, despite the amended act's directive to destroy excess animals. However, since the enactment of the sales directive in 2004, which provided BLM with another means of disposal for these excess animals, Congress has appropriated funds to BLM without the prohibition. BLM has still chosen not to destroy or sell excess animals without limitation because of concerns about public and congressional reaction to the large-scale slaughter of thousands of healthy horses. However, by not destroying or selling them without limitation, BLM is not in compliance with the requirements of the act. Legislation is pending in the 110th Congress that would repeal the 2004 sales directive but not the requirement to destroy excess horses. As of June 2008, budget constraints have forced BLM to reconsider all of its options, including humane destruction and sales without limitations. BLM has not formally considered other possible solutions to deal with the current number of wild horses in long-term holding other than one pilot project in

Wyoming. Some BLM officials suggested that other options are possible, such as placing nonreproducing animals on vacant BLM grazing allotments or on other federal lands, but these actions would require legislative changes.

To improve the management of BLM's Wild Horse and Burro Program, we are recommending that the Secretary of the Interior direct BLM to finalize and issue the new program handbook to ensure that AML determinations are based on consistent factors across HMAs into the future, improve the accuracy of population estimates by continuing to adopt statistically based methods to estimate animal populations, improve public access to data about the welfare of wild horses and burros removed from the range, and develop cost-effective alternatives to caring for wild horses removed from the range in long-term holding facilities. We are also recommending that the Secretary of the Interior direct BLM to initiate discussions with Congress to address BLM's noncompliance with the act. In commenting on a draft of this report, the Department of the Interior concurred with our findings and recommendations and provided several technical clarifications, which we have made as appropriate. Appendix IV presents the Department of the Interior's comment letter.

BACKGROUND

During the 20th century, tens of thousands of wild horses were either killed or captured for slaughter on America's western ranges. Documented abuses suffered by wild horses led concerned individuals and national humane organizations to push for federal protections in the 1950s. Subsequently, Congress passed legislation in 1959 prohibiting the use of aircraft or motor vehicles to capture or kill wild horses or burros on public lands and polluting watering holes on public lands to trap, kill, wound, or maim wild horses or burros. Despite the 1959 act, wild horse exploitation continued, and some questioned whether the population would eventually be eradicated. To protect wild horses and burros, Congress passed additional legislation in 1971 to require the protection and management of wild free-roaming horses and burros on public lands. The 1971 act was amended in 1976, 1978, 1996, and 2004 (see table 1). The 2004 amendments directed BLM to sell, without limitation, excess animals more than 10 years of age or that have been offered unsuccessfully for adoption at least three times.

The passage of the 1971 act changed the way BLM managed wild horses and burros on public lands. Rather than considering them as feral species that caused damage to the rangeland, the agencies had to change their mind-set to protect and manage the animals as an integral part of the ecosystem. One of the first tasks in managing the animals was to determine where they lived and their populations. According to the act, BLM is only authorized to manage wild horses and burros in areas where they were found in 1971.[15] The areas where wild horses and burros were found, largely on public lands managed by the BLM and the Forest Service, as of the date of the act are called herd areas, and they comprise about 53.5 million acres. Once the exact land status and ownership of the herd areas was verified, it was determined that most herd areas were on BLM administered public lands, but some also included private and state-owned in-holdings. The 1971 act states that the Secretaries of the Interior and Agriculture shall arrange for the removal of wild horses and burros that stray onto private land upon notification by the owner.[16]

Table 1. Major Legislation Governing BLM's Wild Horse and Burro Program

Legislation	Date	Major relevant provisions
Public Law 86-234 (Wild Horse Annie Act of 1959)[a]	Sept. 8, 1959	Establishes criminal penalties for using an aircraft or motor vehicle to hunt wild horses or burros on public lands for capturing or killing and for polluting wateringholes on public lands to trap, kill, wound, or maim wild horse or burros.
Public Law 92-195 (Wild Free-Roaming Horses and Burros Act of 1971)[b]	Dec. 15, 1971	Authorizes and directs the Secretaries of the Interior and Agriculture to protect and manage wild horses and burros as components of the public lands to achieve and maintain a thriving natural ecological balance. Authorizes the Secretaries, in areas found to be overpopulated, to order old, sick, or lame animals destroyed in the most humane manner possible and to capture or remove wild horses and burros under humane conditions and care. Authorizes the Secretaries to order wild horses and burros destroyed in the most humane manner possible when such action is deemed necessary to preserve and maintain the habitat in a suitable condition for continued use. The act also establishes criminal penalties for a number of offenses involving wild horses andburros.
Federal Land Policy and Management Act of 1976[c]	Oct. 21, 1976	Directs the Secretary of the Interior to prepare and maintain an inventory of public lands and their resources and other values and to, with public involvement, develop, maintain, and revise land use plans, which provide for the use of public lands. Directs the Secretary to manage the public lands under principles of multiple use and sustained yield. Authorizes the Secretaries of the Interior and Agriculture to contract for the use of helicopters and for using motor vehicles to transport captured animals after a public hearing and in accordance with humane procedures.
Public Rangelands Improvement Act of 1978[d]	Oct. 25, 1978	Directs the Secretaries of the Interior and Agriculture to maintain a current inventory of wild horses and burros on given areas of public lands to determine whether and where overpopulation exists and whether to remove excess animals, the appropriate management levels, and whether appropriate management levels could be achieved by removal or destruction of excess animals or through other options. Directs the Secretaries, upon finding that an overpopulation exists and that action is necessary to remove excess wild horsesand burros, to restore a thriving ecological balance by first destroying old, sick, and lame animals in the most humane manner possible; then humanely capturing and removing wild horses and burros for private maintenance and care for which an adoption demand exists by qualified

		individuals; and then destroying additional excess wild horses and burros in the most humane and cost-efficient manner possible. Authorizes the Secretaries, upon application, to grant title to excess wild horses and burros for which an individual provided humane conditions, treatment, and care for a period of 1 year. Provides that a wild horse or burro is no longer a wild horse and burro for purposes of the 1971 act once title has passed to an individual or in a number of other circumstances. No wild horse and burro or its remains may be sold or transferred for consideration for processing into a commercial product.
Omnibus Parks and Public Lands Management Act of 1996[e]	Nov. 12, 1996	Attempts to clarify the effect of the 1976 amendment, which authorized the Secretaries of the Interior and Agriculture to use helicopters and motor vehicles in the capture and transportation of animals.
Department of the Interior and Related Agencies Appropriations Act, 2005[f]	Dec. 8, 2004	Directs the sale, without limitation, of excess wild horses and burros, or their remains, if the animals are more than 10 years of age or have been offered unsuccessfully for adoption at least three times, until all excess animals are soldor until appropriate management levels are attained. It also provides that wild horses and burros, or their remains, once sold, are no longer wild horses and burros for the purposes of the 1971 act. Exempts animals sold under these provisions from the general prohibition under the 1971 act of processing the remains of wild horses and burros into commercial products.

Source: GAO analysis of laws pertinent to BLM's management of the Wild Horse and Burro Program.

[a] Pub. L. No. 86-234, 73 Stat. 470 (1959) (codified as amended at 18 U.S.C. § 47).

[b] Pub. L. No. 92-195, 85 Stat. 649 (1971) (codified as amended at 16 U.S.C. §§ 1331–1340).

[c] Pub. L. No. 94-579, 90 Stat. 2743 (1976). Specifically, section 404 (90 Stat. 2775) amended the 1971 act (codified as amended at 16 U.S.C. § 1 338a).

[d] Pub. L. No. 95-514, § 14, 92 Stat. 1803, 1808 (1978) (amending 16 U.S.C. §§ 1332–1333).

[e] Pub. L. No. 104-333, Title VIII, § 803, 110 Stat. 4093, 4186 (1996) (amending 16 U.S.C. § 1 338a).

[f] Pub. L. No. 108-447, Div. E, Title I, § 142, 118 Stat. 3039, 3070 (2004) (amending 16 U.S.C. § 1333).

Next, through its land management planning process, BLM designated HMAs within these herd areas. In making HMA designations, BLM determined whether or not the areas where wild horses and burros were found contained adequate forage and water to sustain the herds. BLM also designated some HMAs in such a way as to avoid conflicts with private landowners. Today, BLM is responsible for managing 199 HMAs covering 34.3 million acres across 10 western states (see Figure 1).[17] BLM is currently compiling a history of how BLM field offices made the determination to manage wild horses and burros on the current 34.3 million acres, compared to the 53.5 million acres where they were originally found in 1971. According to BLM officials, they expect the review to be completed by March 2009.

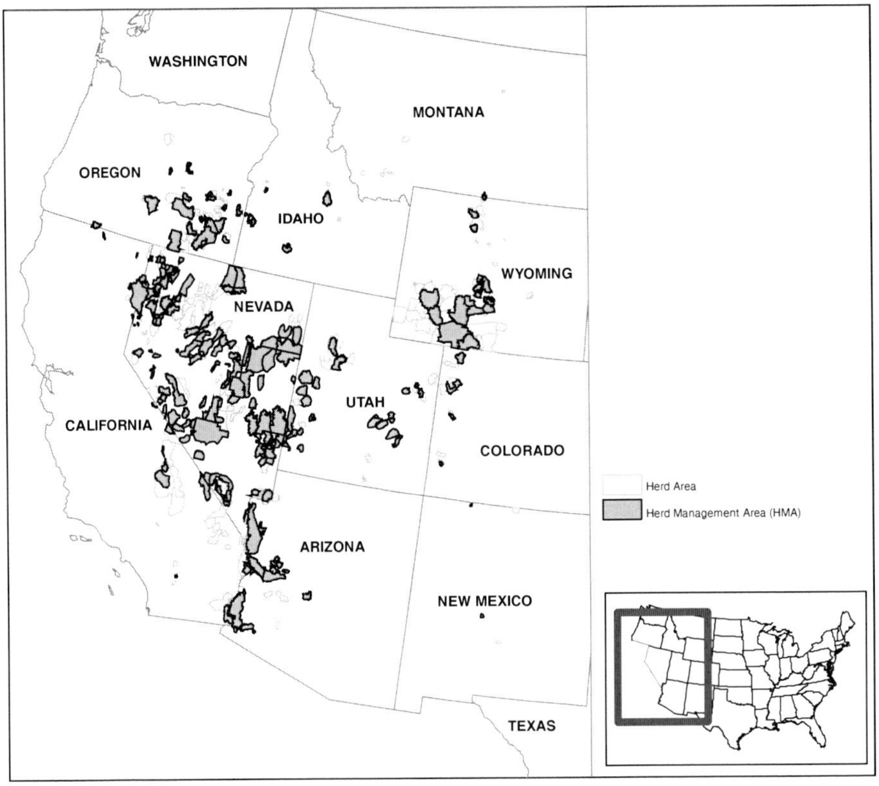

Source: BLM.

Figure 1. BLM Herd Areas and HMAs in the Western United States.

Table 2. Summary Statistics on BLM's Wild Horse and Burro Program, by State, February 2008

State	Number of HMAs	Total AML[a]	Population estimate	HMA acreage		
				BLM acreage	Other acreage	Total acreage
Nevada	102	13,098	16,143	15,772,485	1,695,925	17,468,410
Wyoming	16	3,725	3,439	3,638,330	1,137,121	4,775,451
Arizona	7	1,676	2,173	1,756,086	1,327,777	3,083,863
Oregon	18	2,715	2,473	2,703,409	259,726	2,963,135
Utah	21	2,151	3,096	2,379,850	362,817	2,742,667
California	22	2,237	3,878	1,946,590	471,855	2,418,445
Idaho	6	617	703	377,907	40,287	418,194
Colorado	4	812	933	366,098	38,656	404,754
Montana	1	105	170	28,282	8,865	37,147
New Mexico	2	83	97	24,505	4,107	28,612
Total	**199**	**27,219**	**33,105**	**28,993,542**	**5,347,136**	**34,340,678**

Source: BLM.

[a] This column represents the upper limit of AML according to BLM data.

The number of HMAs and their acreage has changed over time for many different reasons, including BLM land being redesignated as National Park land and declines in forage or water that make an area unsustainable, among others. About half the acreage managed under BLM's Wild Horse and Burro Program is located in Nevada (see table 2). While most of BLM's management activities for wild horses and burros occur within HMAs, BLM is responsible for removing populations of animals that stray onto public lands outside of HMAs, as well as those that stray onto private property.

Wild horses and burros are to be managed as self-sustaining populations of healthy animals in balance with other multiple uses and the productive capacity of their habitat. Because wild horses and burros reproduce at an estimated rate of 20 percent annually and no natural predators remain, except for in a very few isolated HMAs, BLM must actively manage the population of the herds. AML has been defined as the "optimum number of wild horses which results in a thriving natural ecological balance and avoids deterioration of the range."[18] AML determinations can be made in a variety of land planning or decision documents, including, but not limited to, resource management plans, Herd Management Area Plans, and multiple use decision documents. The actual number set through an AML determination is predicated, in part, on (1) the number of acres set-aside for the management of wild horses and burros within a specific resource planning area and (2) the proportion allocation of the available forage allotted for wild horse and burro consumption among other users, such as livestock and wildlife. After these two key multiple use decisions have been made, BLM field offices can then set the actual AML numbers. Available forage is based on range conditions and other data.

BLM's Wild Horse and Burro National Program Office encourages field offices to establish AML as a range with an upper and lower limit.[19] The upper limit of the range equals the maximum number of animals that can be sustained to result in a thriving natural ecological balance and avoid deterioration of the range. The lower limit is generally determined as the number to which a population must be gathered to help ensure the population will not exceed the upper limit of AML within the established gather cycle. For example, if the established gather cycle was 4 years, it would be the number to which a population must be gathered to help ensure the population will not exceed the upper limit of AML within a 4 year time period. BLM strives to maintain a national herd population level that is at the midpoint of AML, where the recently gathered HMAs would be at the lower limit of AML, while those awaiting gathers would be closer to the upper limit of AML. As of February 2008, the upper limit of AML (the cumulative total for each of the 199 HMAs) was approximately 27,219, and the midpoint was about 22,588.[20]

Because AMLs are intended to reflect the population of animals that can be sustainably maintained in an HMA, they are subject to change over time. Changes in AML happen for several reasons, including when acreage is added to or subtracted from an HMA and when changes in rangeland conditions result in improved or reduced forage and water availability sufficient to sustain a certain population level. In the arid ranges where most wild horses and burros are managed, conditions generally do not improve rapidly and have been further degraded by drought conditions that have lasted for over a decade (see Figure 2). The effects of climate change are likely to exacerbate the poor conditions that many HMAs are already experiencing.

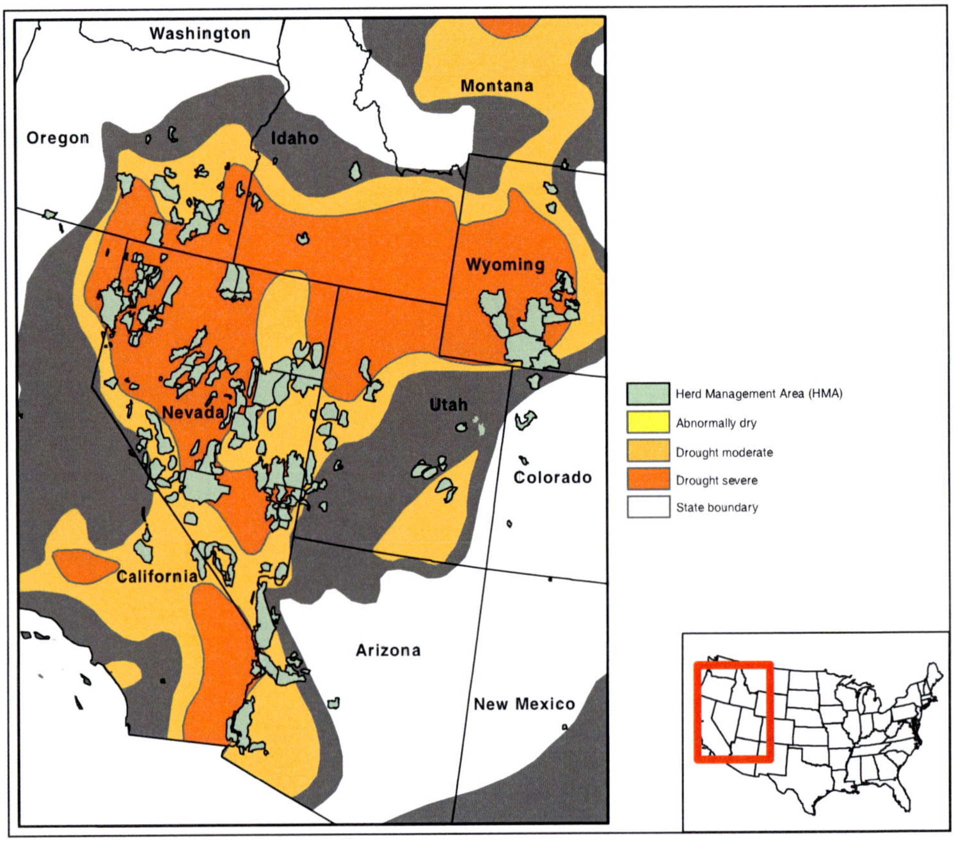

Source: BLM.

Figure 2. Drought Conditions and HMAs, February 2008.

Determining which type of animal is responsible for rangeland damage is important to properly managing an HMA and in determining the number of animals to permit on the range. BLM can control the number of livestock and wild horses and burros to permit on the range, but BLM is not responsible for managing wildlife numbers on the range. Because BLM is not the lead agency responsible for wildlife on public lands, they are to coordinate with state wildlife officials about the forage allocation for wildlife populations. An increase in allocation of any species may cause increased competition for the remaining users of the range, especially under severe conditions. For example, in severe drought conditions, grazing and browsing is concentrated in limited areas near water sources. This intense competition causes heavy use and perhaps depletion of the resources the animals are dependent upon.

Throughout the life of the program, the population of wild horses and burros on the range has generally far exceeded AML. BLM has used the removal of animals from the range as a primary management tool for managing herd sizes. To gather animals for removal, BLM uses private contractors to herd the animals in an HMA into temporary on-site corrals.[21] The animals are primarily gathered using helicopters. In some cases, when gathering smaller numbers of wild horses and burros, BLM officials or contractors will use other trapping techniques, such as bait trapping, to capture the animals. Once collected into the temporary corrals, BLM officials use a selective removal process to determine which of those gathered animals to remove from the HMA.[22] Animals that are not selected are returned to the wild.

When animals are removed from the range, they are taken to short-term holding facilities to receive vaccinations and other treatment prior to either being adopted, sold, or sent to long-term holding. Figure 3 depicts BLM's management of wild horses and burros on and off of the range.

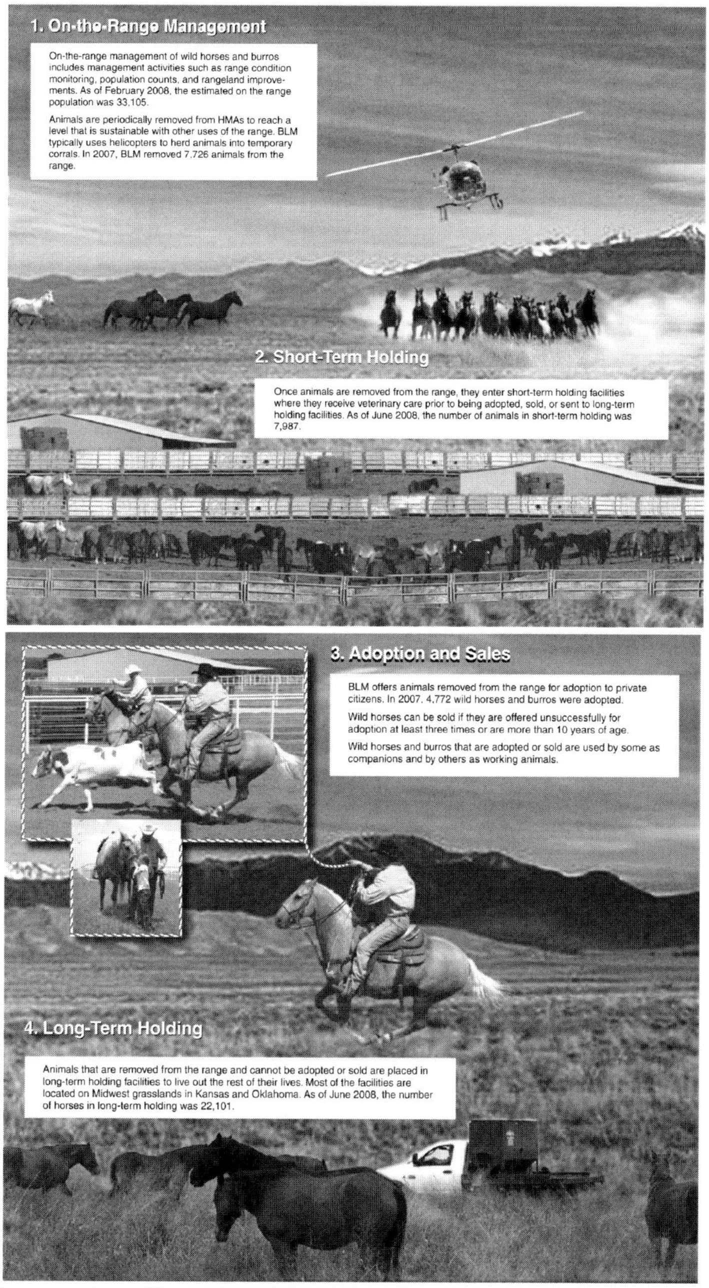

Sources: GAO (photos, photo illustration), BLM (photos).

Figure 3. BLM Management of Wild Horses and Burros on and off of the Range.

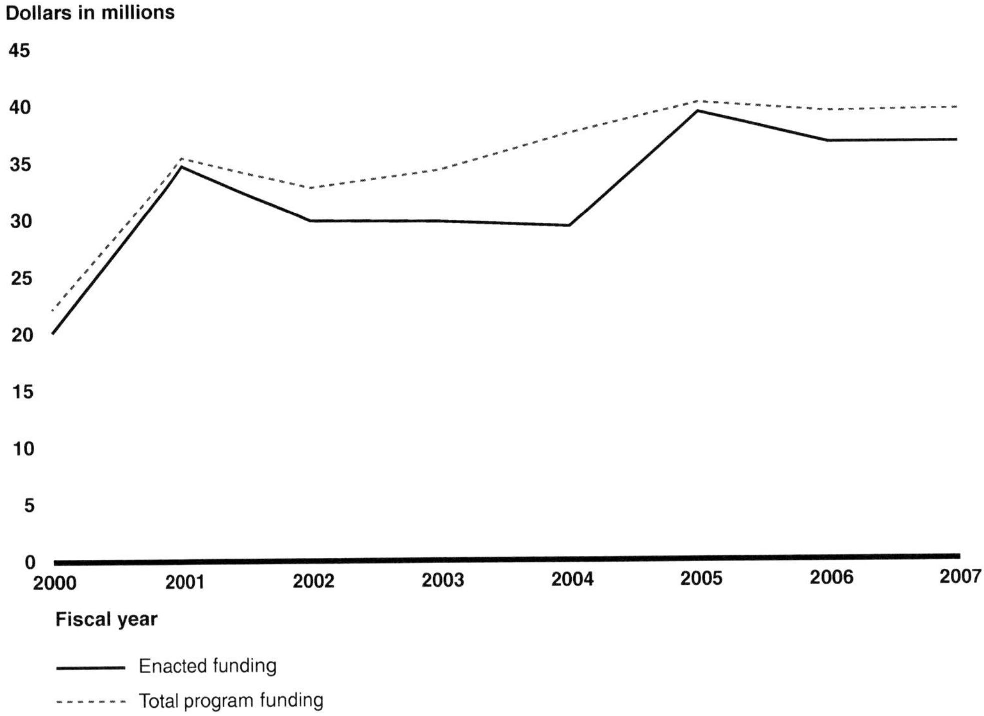

Source: BLM.

Note: The enacted funding level, as reported by BLM, is the amount allocated from congressional appropriations minus rescissions for the Wild Horse and Burro Program. Total program funding represents the sum of the enacted funding; reprogrammed funding; and funding from other sources, such as reimbursement for BLM's management of parts of the Forest Service's Wild Horse and Burro Program.

Figure 4. BLM's Wild Horse and Burro Program Funding, Fiscal Years 2000 through 2007.

For fiscal year 2001, BLM requested a budget increase for the program as part of a major initiative to reach the upper limit of AML by 2005.[23] Subsequently, program funding allocated from congressional appropriations—what the agency refers to as "enacted funding"—increased from $19.8 million in fiscal year 2000 to $34.4 million in fiscal year 2001, an increase of $14.6 million. In 2002, enacted funding for the program was $29.6 million, about $10 million over the 2000 congressional funding level. After reassessing the initiative in 2004, BLM estimated it needed an additional $10.5 million on top of their enacted funding level of $29.1 million in fiscal year 2004 to meet its revised goal of meeting the midpoint of AML by 2006. In fiscal year 2005, enacted funding was increased about $10 million for a total of $39 million in fiscal year 2005 (see Figure 4). The President's 2008 budget requested $32 million for the program, about $4 million less than enacted funding for fiscal year 2007.

LM HAS MADE PROGRESS IN SETTING AND MEETING AML, BUT GUIDANCE IS LACKING AND MEETING AML HAS PROVEN DIFFICULT

BLM has made significant progress in setting and meeting AML for the HMAs. As of February 2008, BLM has set AML for 197 out of 199 HMAs. Most of the field offices we surveyed considered similar factors in determining AML, such as rangeland conditions and climate data; however, BLM has not provided specific formal guidance to the field offices on how to set AML. BLM has been working on revising the program's handbook to provide such guidance since 2006. With increased retirements, field offices reported losing the experienced personnel most familiar with the informal practice of determining AML. Until BLM finalizes the handbook or issues other guidance, it cannot ensure that the factors considered in future revisions of AML determinations are consistent across HMAs. At the national level, BLM reported that it was closer to meeting AML in 2007 than in any other year since AMLs were documented in 1984. Specifically, as of February 2007, BLM estimated the population at 28,563, which was about 1,000 animals over AML. To reach this level, BLM has reduced the nationwide population in the wild by about 40 percent since 2000. However, the population estimates are higher for 2008, and BLM has not met its goal of meeting AML for each HMA. The fact that not all HMAs have met AML remains a concern because of the damage excessive populations can cause on the range. Twenty of 26 field officials we surveyed told us that conducting gathers to remove excess animals is among their top challenges to maintaining AML because delayed gathers can cause animal populations to quickly exceed AML. In our 1990 report we concluded that BLM's decisions on the number of wild horses and burros to remove were made without adequate information about range carrying capacity or the impact of the animals on range conditions. In August 2005, BLM updated its formal policy on gathers and removals and specified the key factors that should be considered in the decision making process. The extent to which BLM has actually met AML depends on the accuracy of BLM's wild horse and burro population counts. Nineteen of the 26 field officials we surveyed used a method that consistently undercounts animals and does not provide a statistical range of population estimates. Alternative counting methods may be more expensive, but undercounting a population can lead to overpopulation and costlier gathers in future years.

BLM has Set AML for 197 out of 199 HMAs, but no Formal Guidance Exists on how to Establish AML

BLM has made significant progress in setting AML using rangeland monitoring data for the HMAs. As of February 2008, BLM has set AML for 197 out of 199 HMAs, compared to 2002 when about two-thirds of HMAs had set AML.[24] Prior to 1984, many of the initial AMLs were not based on rangeland data but on factors such as initial herd population counts or administrative convenience. For example, the original AML established for Beaty's Butte HMA in Oregon in 1977 was based on the number of horses found in that area on December 15, 1971. In Wyoming, AMLs for about one-third of the HMAs were based on agreements with local grazing interests because they owned private lands that were interspersed with BLM lands where wild horses were found in 1971. Only 10 out of the 26 field offices we surveyed identified the use of rangeland data to determine their initial AMLs. But since 1984, in accordance with the *Dahl v. Clark* decision, BLM officials told us that field managers have generally based AML decisions on monitoring data and an in-depth analysis.[25] Most of the current AMLs for the 199 HMAs were set after 1984 (see table 3). Although some current AMLs were set many years ago, they are generally reviewed every 4 years or so as part of the recurring process to gather and remove excess animals. If during this process, and through monitoring, it is determined that an AML is no longer appropriate, field offices will consider changing it. For example, table 17 in appendix III shows how the current AMLs for the 26 HMAs in our sample have been changed, as applicable, since they were initially set.

Most of the field offices we surveyed considered similar factors in determining AML.[26] According to BLM National Program Office officials, field office staff should consider at least four factors in making AML determinations—climatic data, utilization data, actual use data, and trend data. Climate data measures the amount of precipitation within a specific area. In addition, temperature and wind data may be collected to evaluate the effect of climate on vegetation; utilization data measures the percent of forage consumed by livestock, wild horses and burros, wildlife, and insects during a specified period; actual use data is the number of grazing animals that used an area within a certain amount of time; and trend data measures the direction of change in ecological status or resource rating observed over time. Our survey results indicate that these four key AML determination factors were considered by some, but not all, of the BLM field offices responsible for setting AML for our sample of 26 HMAs (see Table 4).

Almost all of the field offices considered trend (25) and utilization (23) data, but only 19 considered climate and actual use data for livestock, while 14 considered actual use data for wildlife (see Table 5).

Table 3. Years in Which Current AMLs Were Set for BLM's 199 HMAs

Years in which current AMLs were set	**Number of HMAs**
1975–1979[a]	2
1980–1984	13
1985–1989	13
1990–1994	45
1995–1999	32
2000–2004	68
2005–2008	24
Not yet set	2
Total	**199**

Source: GAO analysis of BLM data.

Note: Although an AML may have been set years ago, they are generally reviewed every 4 years or so as part of the reoccurring process to gather and remove excess animals.

[a] AML determinations were first required by the Public Rangelands Improvement Act of 1978.

Table 4. Extent to Which BLM Field Office Staff Considered Each of the Four Key Factors in Making the Most Recent AML Determination for Surveyed Field Offices

Number of the four key factors considered	Number of BLM field offices
4	16
3	6
2	2
1	1
0	1
Total	**26**

Source: GAO survey results.

Table 5. Factors Considered by BLM Field Office Staff in Making the Most Recent AML Determinations for Surveyed Field Offices

Factor	Considered	Not considered	Don't know	Not applicable	Blank
Factors BLM officials told us should be considered					
Trend	25	1	0	0	0
Utilization	23	2	1	0	0
Climate data	19	3	4	0	0
Actual use: livestock	19	2	2	3	0
Actual use: wildlife	14	5	6	1	0
Other factors considered					
Carrying capacity	23	1	2	0	0
Census/inventory	22	2	2	0	0
Water resources	21	3	2	0	0
Stakeholder influence	20	2	4	0	0
Production	19	2	5	0	0
Herd health	19	4	3	0	0
Genetic viability	16	6	3	1	0
Recreational use	14	6	3	3	0
Cultural resources	12	6	5	2	1
Archeological resources	12	6	5	2	1
Livestock agreements	11	4	7	4	0
Human safety issues	8	8	2	8	0
Community expansion	4	8	2	12	0
Court order	2	5	2	17	0
Mineral extraction	3	10	2	11	0
Other factors	7	1	0	1	17

Source: GAO survey results.

In addition to the four factors mentioned by BLM National Program Office officials, field offices considered other factors to help make their AML determinations, including census inventory, water resource availability, herd health, and unique local conditions. For instance, in Arizona, one field office reduced the AML for burros on an HMA because they found that burros were foraging on the same willows critical to the survival of the endangered Southwestern Willow Flycatcher.[27]

In determining AML, field office staff must also consider rangeland conditions for wild horses and burros in conjunction with other users of the range, including livestock and wildlife. Determining which species is responsible for rangeland damage is an important task to properly managing the HMA and in determining the number of wild horses and burros to permit on the range. For example, if field staff determine that cattle are primarily responsible for damaging an area, they may pursue several management options, including fencing out cattle, reducing the number of cattle, or changing the time of year cattle are allowed to graze in a particular area. BLM lacks similar management techniques to control wild horse and burro use due to their free-roaming nature. BLM's direct management actions are limited to dealing with livestock and wild horses and burros, since individual states are responsible for managing wildlife.

We recognized the difficulty in distinguishing the difference between impacts that wild horses and burros have on the range versus other users in our 1990 report.[28] Some advocacy groups have criticized BLM because they believe that BLM unfairly faults wild horse and burros for damage to the range to justify their removal and reductions in AML. Several BLM officials told us ascribing range impacts can be difficult, but 20 out of the 26 field offices that we surveyed said they had a procedure in place do so. When the damage is caused by all the user groups or when the damage can not be attributed to a specific user group, BLM will generally make across-the-board reductions in the number of animals allowed on the range based on the historic proportion of each user group on the range. For example, if wild horses and burros historically accounted for 10 percent of the forage consumption on the range, then wild horses and burros would bear 10 percent of the necessary reductions.

BLM has also made steady reductions in cattle grazing on BLM land as drought conditions in much of the West have worsened, resulting in the reduction of forage and water availability. For example, in Nevada, the state that manages for the greatest number of wild horses, permitted livestock use was reduced from about 2.5 million animal unit months in 1990 to a little over 2 million in 2006.[29] The actual use during this same period, however, decreased from 1.8 million animal unit months to 1.2 million.

In addition to the factors considered in making AML determinations, the age of the data, or how current it is, can also be important. The meaning of "current" data collection depends on the ecosystem and may vary across HMAs. BLM national program officials explained that data used to support AML decisions should be collected on a frequent basis. In general, they told us climate, utilization, and actual use data should be collected annually and trend data should be analyzed and reviewed within 4 years of setting AML. However, of the respondents who provided the age for data used, fewer than half collected their data for actual use for livestock and wildlife within 1 year of their AML determination; half collected their data for utilization within 1 year of the determination; and more than half collected their data for climate within 1 year of the determination. Fifteen of the 19 respondents who provided the age for data used considered trend data within 4 years of the determination (see table 6).

Table 6. Age of Data Used to Make Current AML Determinations for Surveyed Field Offices

Factor	Age of the data					
	1 year	2 years	3 years	4 years	5-10 years	11 yearsor older
Factors BLM officials told us should be considered						
Trend	8	3	1	3	4	0
Utilization	9	2	1	3	3	0
Climate data	9	2	0	2	2	0
Actual use: livestock	6	3	0	2	3	0
Actual use: wildlife	5	1	0	2	2	1
Other factors considered						
Carrying capacity	7	3	0	2	5	1
Census inventory	13	1	1	2	1	0
Water inventory	11	2	0	2	1	0
Production	6	1	0	2	3	2
Herd health	11	1	0	3	1	0
Genetic viability	8	0	0	3	1	0

Source: GAO survey results.

Note: Some field offices that considered the factors listed in this table did not provide a year in which the data was collected.

Although field offices use many factors to make their AML determinations, BLM has no guidance or policy about the specific factors they must consider in determining AML. This is in contrast to the BLM policy that exists for a similar type of analysis that is conducted for removals. According to BLM's 2005 gather policy, the determination to remove animals must be supported by the following factors: climatic data, utilization data, actual use data, trend data, and current census data.[30] While 22 out of 26 BLM field offices responded that the data used to make their AML determination were moderate to very sufficient, several BLM officials told us that with increased retirements, field offices are losing the experienced personnel most familiar with the informal practice of determining AML. Therefore, without clear guidance, BLM cannot ensure that the factors considered in future revisions of AML determinations will be consistent across HMAs. To make the informal AML determination process official and to help ensure consistency among BLM field offices, BLM officials have been working on drafting a new handbook for the program since 2006, which specifies the factors field offices should use in making AML determinations.[31] Due to higher priorities and limited resources, the handbook is still in draft form and is undergoing final revision. BLM officials told us they expect the handbook to be completed in fall 2008.

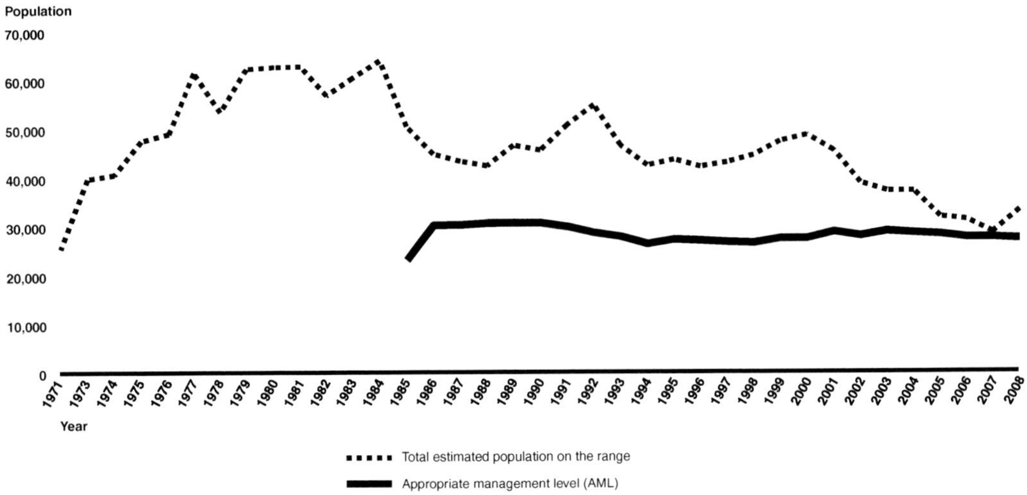

Source: BLM.

Note: All population levels are estimated based on aerial surveys that likely undercount the number of animals on the range. In 2000, BLM changed the time frame for its population counts from October 1 through September 30 of every year to March 1 through February 28 or 29 of every year. For AML levels prior to 1984, BLM was unable to provide estimated figures. For AML levels from 1984 through 1999, the figures are estimated and they do not necessarily reflect the upper limit of AML; from 2000 onward, the AML figures represent the upper limit of AML.

Figure 5. Estimated Population of Wild Horses and Burros on the Range.

BLM has Made Significant Progress toward Meeting AML, but some HMAs Remain far over AML

Since 2000, BLM has made significant progress toward meeting AML. At the national level, BLM was closer to meeting AML in 2007 than in any other year since 1984 (when AML levels were first reported by BLM), with a population of 28,563, or about 1,000 animals over the upper limit of AML (see Figure 5). Meeting AML has been a challenge for most of the lifetime of the program. In 1985, in reporting on the Department of the Interior and related agencies' appropriations, the Senate Committee on Appropriations recommended more than tripling the program's funding above the original budgeted amounts to, according to the committee, permit BLM to maintain nearly 14,000 animals in corrals through the end of fiscal year 1986 and to remove 17,000 excess animals during fiscal year 1986.[32] The program's funding was tripled in fiscal year 1986, and with the increased funding, BLM removed 18,959 excess animals. In fiscal year 2001, BLM began implementing a 4-year strategy to aggressively remove animals from the range to reach the upper limit of AML by 2005. However, just before initiating the strategy—which relied heavily on specific assumptions about the number of animals removed, adopted, and held in short-term and long-term holding—emergency drought and fire conditions called for the removal of wild horses and burros in numbers far greater than anticipated. These additional removals and decreases in adoption targets changed BLM's assumptions and made it clear the agency would not be able to meet the targets set forth in their plan. In 2004, BLM again revisited targets and management options that would help them to achieve and maintain the midpoint of AML by 2006. Over the past several years, the program is closer to meeting AML as a result of increases in the number of wild horses and burros removed from the range, but it continues to face challenges in maintaining that level. According to BLM data, the population now exceeds the upper limit of AML by an estimated 5,886 animals. BLM attributes most of the increase in population to more accurate population census counts.

While the national statistics appear to indicate that BLM is close to meeting its goal, it is important to note that, under the act, BLM is required to maintain HMAs at a level that is at or below the upper limit of AML. To stay below the upper limit of AML, HMAs should be gathered to the lower limit of AML approximately every 3 to 5 years. However, only 7 of the 26 BLM field offices we surveyed said they were typically able to gather to this low level. When animals are not gathered to the low level of AML, a population can quickly rise well above the upper limit of AML. Fewer than half (10) of the field offices surveyed said they were usually able to manage the population of wild horses and burros on their HMAs within the limits of AML. Fifteen field offices said they managed populations that were typically above AML.

We are not reporting in detail on the extent to which individual HMAs have met AML because we do not believe that BLM's data are precise enough to accurately make such a determination. BLM's estimates of the number of HMAs that are at or below AML may be overstated because, for reporting purposes, BLM considers the HMAs where the population is not more than 10 percent over the upper limit of the AML to be at AML. BLM officials told us that this is done to account for those HMAs that may slightly exceed AML. For example, in 2008, BLM reported that 61 of the 102 HMAs in Nevada were at or below AML. Without the 10 percent adjustment factor, we calculated that 52 HMAs were at or below AML. Because of this adjustment factor and questions about the accuracy of BLM's animal counting methods, we concluded that the data on whether or not individual HMAs had met AML were not sufficiently reliable to report because an error of plus or minus one or two animals could change the status of an HMA from being under or over AML. Aside from the precise issue of whether or not an HMA is within or over AML, it is clear from the data that some HMAs are significantly over AML. For example, as of February 2008, BLM reported that 87 HMAs were over AML. About half of these HMAs were over AML by 50 percent or less, about a quarter were over AML by between 51 and 100 percent, and about another quarter of the HMAs were over AML by more than 100 percent.

Populations that exceed AML can harm the health of the range. For example, in 2004, the Calico HMA in Nevada exceeded AML by about 200 percent. The herds were found to concentrate in sensitive areas, affecting the threatened Lahontan cutthroat trout and contributing to the nonattainment of grazing allotment objectives and standards for rangeland health.[33] As of February 2008, the wild horse population in this HMA exceeded the upper limit of AML by 160 percent. The excess population levels and continued drought are expected to continue to negatively impact sensitive riparian areas relied upon by the Lahontan cutthroat trout. The overpopulation of wild horses and burros on the range may negatively impact herd health, rangeland health, and livestock and wildlife that depend on the range. An over-obligation of the vegetative resources can result in declines in the healthy vegetative condition that may take years to recover. See figure 6 for our survey results on the possible negative impacts of populations that exceed the upper limits of AML.

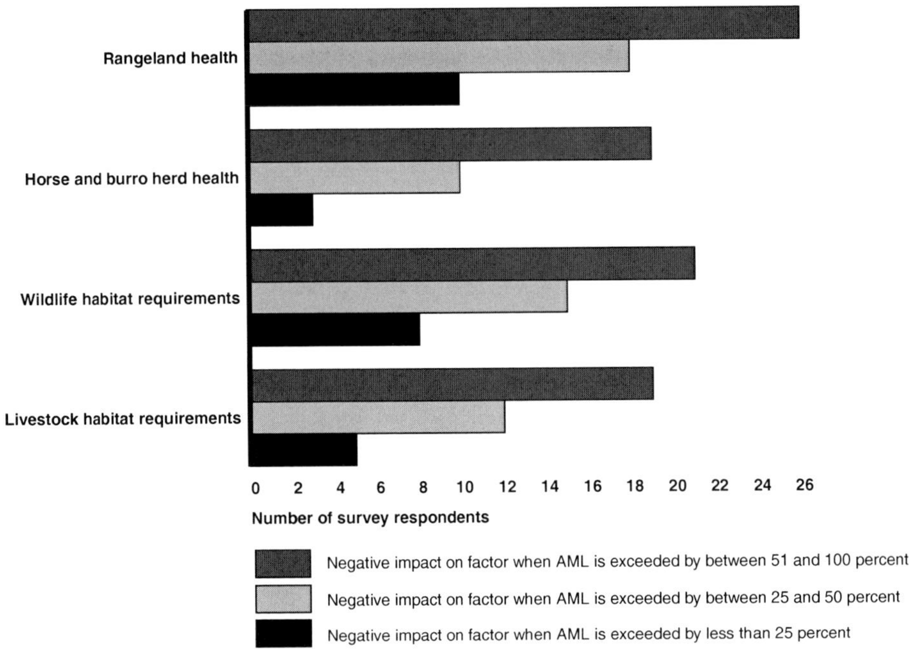

Source: GAO analysis of survey data. Note: We asked survey respondents to identify the impact (positive, slightly positive, no impact, slightly negative, and negative) that populations that exceed the upper limit of AML would have on the four factors above. The figure is a graphic depiction of survey respondents who reported negative impacts when populations exceed AML. See appendix III for the number of survey respondents who reported positive, slightly positive, no impact, or slightly negative impacts when the upper limit of AML is exceeded by a certain percentage.

Figure 6. Number of Field Offices Who Reported Negative Impacts When Populations Exceed the Upper Limit of AML.

In addition to the effects on the range, overpopulation in HMAs also results in costlier gathers because a greater number of animals would have to be removed to maintain AML in future years.

Although there has been an increased effort to meet AML, there have been many challenges in meeting and maintaining that level. Twenty of the 26 field officials we surveyed identified limitations to gathers to remove excess animals as one of their top challenges to meeting or maintaining AML. One limitation identified by these respondents included limited funding available to conduct gathers. Another limitation identified by respondents was unplanned gathers that alter the gather schedule as resources are directed to HMAs in critical need. Reasons for unplanned gathers include escalating problems and emergencies. An HMA with an escalating problem is defined as an area where deteriorating rangeland conditions, such as declining availability of forage or water, will negatively affect animal condition and rangeland health. Emergency situations are unexpected situations that threaten the immediate health of wild horses and burros or their habitat, such as fire, disease, or other catastrophic events.

In addition to using gathers and removals to manage the population on the range, BLM may also use fertility treatment to manage the reproductive rates of wild horses. BLM is using this tool on a limited number of HMAs. However, some animal fertility researchers and wild horse advocates believe that this tool should be used more widely. They say that unless the reproductive rate is curtailed, the need to gather a large number of animals from the range will continue. See appendix II for more information about BLM's use of this treatment.

BLM has Established a Formal Policy on Gathers and Removals that Specifies the Key Factors that should be Considered in the Decision Making Process

Removals are used as a primary method for managing wild horse and burro populations on the range; however, the data used to support these removal decisions have been criticized. Specifically, our 1990 report concluded that BLM's decisions on the number of wild horses and burros to remove were made without adequate information about range carrying capacity or the impact of the animals on range conditions.[34] In August 2005, BLM issued an update to their 2002 policy on gathers that determinations to support gathers and removals must be based on a National Environmental Policy Act analysis and a gather plan that consider five key factors—utilization, trend, actual use, climatic data, and current census.[35] Eleven of the 26 field offices we surveyed considered all five key factors in their most recent gather plan (see table 7). However, many of these field offices conducted their most recent gathers prior to the issuance of the 2005 policy that specified which factors to consider in their decision making process. Specifically, 11 field offices conducted their most recent gathers between 1990 and 2005. Additionally, some field offices' most recent gathers were conducted as a result of an emergency situation. In those cases, a field office may not have had enough time to consider all five criteria due to the critical time response necessary to remove the animals.[36]

Regardless of when the most recent gathers were conducted, 25 of the 26 field offices we surveyed considered the data used to support their removals for specific HMAs as moderately to very sufficient. See table 8 for the number of field offices that considered each of the factors we asked about in our survey.

Table 7. Extent to Which BLM Field Office Staff Considered Each of the Five Key Factors in Making Their Most Recent Gather Determination

Number of the five key factors considered	Number of respondents
5	11
4	4
3	5
2	1
1	4
0	1
Total	**26**

Source: GAO survey results.

Table 8. Factors Considered by Field Offices in Decisions to Gather Wild Horses and Burros from the Range

Factor	Considered	Not considered	Don't know	Not applicable	Blank
Factors that should be considered					
Census/inventory	24	2	0	0	0
Utilization	21	3	1	0	1
Climate data	19	5	1	0	1
Trend	16	6	2	1	1
Actual use: livestock	11	8	2	4	1
Actual use: wildlife	8	10	3	4	1
Other factors considered					
Herd health	21	4	1	0	0
Carrying capacity	17	6	2	0	1
Water resources	16	7	1	0	2
Stakeholder influence	16	3	3	2	2
Production	12	8	4	1	1
Livestock agreements	12	6	1	5	2
Cultural resources	12	7	1	4	2
Archeological resources	12	8	1	3	2
Genetic viability	11	11	2	1	1
Recreational use	8	8	1	7	2
Other factors	8	0	1	3	14
Human safety issues	7	10	1	6	2
Court order	3	5	1	14	3
Mineral extraction	3	9	1	11	2
Community expansion	1	11	1	11	2

Source: GAO survey results.

Unlike our previous report, which stated that data to justify removals was outdated, most respondents who provided the year in which their data was collected indicated that their data was current as of the year of their most recent gather or less than 4 years old (see table 9).

Half of the survey respondents identified impediments to conducting gathers as a major challenge in managing their HMAs to achieve healthy herd populations that are in balance with the range and other multiple uses. Only 7 of the 26 field offices surveyed said that they were able to typically gather to their lower limits of AML. While several BLM officials explained that gathers can be delayed as a result of funding restrictions or emergency gather priorities, only four of the field offices surveyed indicated that their most recent gather was delayed.

Table 9. Age of Data Used by Field Offices to Determine the Need for Most Recent Gather

Factor	Age of the data					
	1 year	2 years	3 years	4 years	5-10 years	11 yearsor older
Factors that should be considered						
Census/inventory	14	2	3	0	0	0
Utilization	13	1	0	1	0	0
Climate data	15	0	0	1	0	0
Trend	8	1	1	1	2	0
Actual use: livestock	10	0	0	0	0	0
Actual use: wildlife	7	0	0	0	0	0
Other factors considered						
Herd health	11	2	1	1	0	0
Carrying capacity	6	1	1	0	1	2
Water resources	8	0	0	1	0	0
Production	6	1	0	1	0	0
Genetic viability	1	1	1	2	1	0

Source: GAO survey results.

Research and Experience have Shown that BLM's On-the-Range Population Estimates Are too Low

Accurate animal population counts are critical to BLM's ability to properly manage wild horse and burro herds and in determining whether AML targets were met. However, many field offices use a population counting method—the direct-count method—that researchers consider inaccurate. This method generally calls for one person to count each animal they spot from an airplane or helicopter. According to researchers, it consistently undercounts animals and does not provide a statistical range of estimates. Nineteen of the 26 field officials we surveyed used the direct-count method for conducting their most recent census.

Regardless of which method is used, counting wild horses and burros can be challenging, particularly when the animals are obscured by trees or when the rangeland is covered with snow. Because counting poses such challenges, researchers are investigating alternative counting methods to assist BLM in collecting accurate population data to form statistically valid population estimates.[37] Each method the researchers are evaluating includes some range of statistical error, whereas direct count only reports the raw number spotted on the ground. Researchers believe that the most effective method will likely be a combination of two or more counting techniques. BLM's population counts of wild horses and burros have long been questioned by managers and advocacy groups alike. By employing alternative methods that account for a range of error, BLM would have a more defensible way of determining population estimates. In the most recent 2008 BLM population estimates, for example, population counts exceeded those in 2007 by approximately 4,500 animals. As a result, on a nationwide level, BLM is once again well over the upper limit of AML, which brings into question earlier population estimates and whether or not those previous years were as close to meeting AML as once thought. BLM is working with the Department of the Interior's U.S. Geological Survey's Fort Collins Science Center and the Colorado State University to develop these methods to achieve greater accuracy in population counts. Some BLM offices have begun to employ some of these methods. For example, in Arizona, managers use the simultaneous double-count method to improve population counts and avoid underestimating burro populations. Some field offices, however, are reluctant to use alternate counting methods because they are concerned that they would require too much additional staff or would be too expensive. Researchers agree that other methods may be slightly more expensive, given the greater number of staff needed.

When a population is undercounted, BLM is likely to remove fewer animals than is needed to control overpopulation. For example, in 2002, a direct count was used to census the wild horse population located on the Jackson Mountain HMA in northern Nevada, an area that has been affected by severe drought. When a gather was conducted in 2003, staff believed they removed the adequate number of wild horses to reach AML. Funds to conduct their scheduled census in 2006 were not available, and BLM was unable to conduct its population count until the summer of 2007. It was at this point that staff realized that their 2002 census was incorrect and that they miscalculated the population in 2007 by approximately 640 wild horses. They found that the actual population in 2007 was about five times greater than what they determined was sustainable. In the winter of 2007, BLM began to monitor water availability more regularly. The BLM field staff member who managed that HMA told us that although the herd condition was weakened, the horses did not appear to be in extremely poor condition. Nevertheless, more than 150 of the wild horses removed from this HMA died in a short-term holding facility due to disease that was able to overtake the animals in their weakened state.

Declining Adoptions and Sales have Increased the Need for Short-Term and Long-Term Holding Facilities, and Holding Costs have Increased

The number of wild horses and burros removed from the range is far greater than the number adopted or sold. Since 2001, about 74,000 animals have been removed from the range, while only about 46,400 have been adopted or sold. This has resulted in significant spending increases due to a greater number of animals in short- and long-term holding. Thirty-six percent fewer wild horses and burros were adopted in 2007, compared to average adoption rates in the 1990s—a trend BLM officials attribute to the decrease in adoption demand and increasing hay and fuel costs. Since 2004, when BLM was directed to sell excess wild horses and burros without limitation, BLM has sold about 2,700 animals—far fewer than expected, despite the low average selling price of $15. As of June 2008, BLM was holding 30,088 animals in short- and long-term holding facilities, compared with the estimated 9,807 held in 2001. To accommodate the increase in animals removed from the range and the decline in adoptions and sales, BLM has increased the number of short- and long-term holding facilities. This has resulted in an increase in spending for short- and long-term holding facilities.

Adoption Rates have Declined since the 1990s, and the 2004 Sale Directive Generally has not been Used

BLM has historically managed wild horses and burros removed from the range through adoptions to the general public. Adoption has been regarded as the most economical way to provide humane long-term care to animals that have been removed from the range. In the 1990s, the number of animals removed from the range was about equal to the number of animals adopted. The average number of animals adopted each year in the 1990s was about 7,500. Since 2000, the number of animals removed has outpaced the number of animals adopted or sold due to an increase in removals and a steady decline in adoption demand and sales. Since 2001, about 74,000 animals have been removed from the range, compared to about 46,400 adopted or sold. The average number removed annually from 2001 to 2007 was about 10,600, compared to the average adoption rate of about 6,300 annually. According to BLM's 2004 Report to Congress, at least 7,000 adoptions were needed annually to assist in achieving and maintaining AML. However, only about 4,700 animals were adopted in 2007. Although BLM has increased efforts to market adoptions, demand continues to decline for wild horses, even though the price for adopting them has remained at the minimum fee of $125 since 1997.[38] BLM officials attribute the steady wild horse adoption decline in recent years to increases in hay and fuel costs associated with horse care, the large number of domesticated horses that are currently flooding the adoption market,[39] a general urbanization of rural areas, and a shift toward other forms of recreation. For example, according to one official, individuals who once had corrals with two or three horses may now own one horse and four all-terrain vehicles. Figure 7 compares the number of wild horses and burros removed from the range with the number adopted from 1989 through 2007.

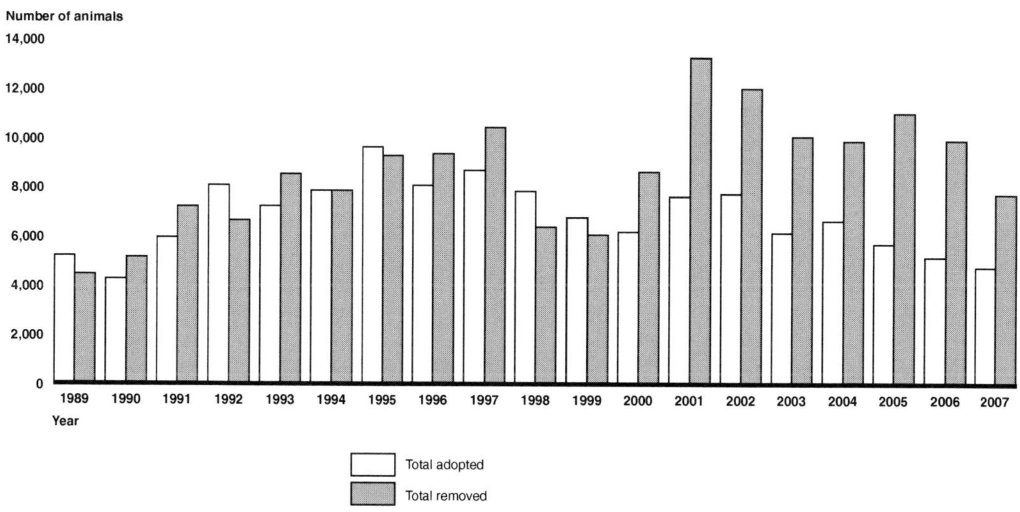

Source: BLM.

Figure 7. Comparison of Removed and Adopted Wild Horses and Burros, 1989 through 2007.

Table 10. Number of Wild Horses and Burros Sold under the December 8, 2004, Sales Directive

Year	Numbersold
2005	1,468
2006	645
2007	420
2008[a]	211
Total	**2,744**

Source: BLM.
[a] As of June 2008.

One alternative for managing unadoptable excess wild horses and burros, as provided for by the 2004 amendment to the 1971 act, is to sell the animals "without limitation." The act directs BLM to offer excess animals for sale that are more than 10 years old or that have been offered unsuccessfully for adoption at least three times. At the time of the amendment, BLM estimated that approximately 8,400 animals were eligible for sale. To date, BLM has sold only about 2,700 animals—far fewer than originally expected, despite the low average selling price in 2006 of $15 (see table 10).

In 2005, the first sale was made to a wild horse protection group in Wyoming who purchased 200 horses that would otherwise have likely ended up in long-term holding under BLM's care. A few other animals that were sold, however, ultimately ended up in slaughterhouses. To reduce the likelihood that a buyer would purchase these animals and then sell them for slaughter, BLM changed its sales process to require buyers to sign a "statement of intent" that they do not intend to sell the animals for slaughter. This limitation, as well as a decrease in demand, has contributed to the small number of sales.

BLM Manages 30,088 Animals in an Increasing Number of Short-Term and Long-Term Holding Facilities, and Holding Costs have Increased

As of June 2008, BLM was holding a combined 30,088 animals in short-term and long-term holding facilities, compared to 9,807 animals in 2001. To accommodate the increase in animals needing care once removed from the range, the number of short-term and long-term holding facilities has increased. Spending on combined short-term and long-term holding has also increased from about $7 million in 2000 to about $20.9 million in 2007. From 2001 through 2008, the number of short-term holding facilities increased from 14 to 24,[40] and the number of animals held in these facilities increased from 6,514 animals to 7,987 by June 2008. These holding facilities provide the animals with vaccinations and other care prior to their being adopted, sold, or sent to long-term holding. The average cost of animals in short-term holding increased from $3.00 per horse per day in 2001 to $5.08 per horse per day in 2008. From 2000 to 2001, the cost for short-term holding increased from $6.4 million to $11.2 million. From 2001 through 2007, the cost remained relatively stable, but for 2008, costs are anticipated to increase to $16.2 million. According to several BLM officials, the escalating cost for caring for animals in short-term holding is primarily a result of the dramatic increase in hay and fuel prices from 2007 to 2008. For example, hay prices for one short-term holding facility in Nevada increased from about $160 per ton in 2007 to almost $300 per ton in 2008. Decreases in adoption and sales and a lack of capacity in long-term holding has not only increased the number of animals held in short-term holding, but has also increased the time animals are held there. According to one state official, animals in his state spent 45 to 60 days in short-term holding facilities in the late 1990s. Beginning in 2000, this official told us, it was not uncommon to hold animals for more than a year. Nationwide, according to BLM, the average length of stay in short-term holding in 2008 has been 210 days. This is far longer than the 90 days BLM projected animals would spend in short-term holding in their 2001 initiative to meet AML.

Table 11. Number of Wild Horses in Long-Term Holding, by Year, Since 2000

Year	**Number of facilities**	**Capacity**	**Number of horsesin long-term holding**
2000	1	2,000	1,500
2001	3	6,000	3,293
2002	5	10,000	7,311
2003	7	14,000	10,122
2004	7	14,000	13,151
2005	9	20,600	15,379
2006	8	19,700	18,198
2007	10	21,800	19,652
2008[a]	11	22,100	22,101

Source: BLM.

[a] As of June 2008.

Table 12. BLM Long-Term Holding Facilities, June 2008

Name of facility	**Location**	**Year(s) animals first held in facility**	**Capacity**	**Horsesheld**
Bartlesville	Oklahoma	1989	2,300	2,066
Catoosa	Oklahoma	2001	2,000	2,042
Teterville East	Kansas	2001	2,200	1,913
Teterville West	Kansas	2002	2,200	2,531
Foraker	Oklahoma	2003	2,500	2,507
Pawhuska	Oklahoma	2003–2004	3,400	3,646
Grenola	Kansas	2004	2,200	2,269
Hulah	Oklahoma	2004	2,200	2,203
Herd	Oklahoma	2007	1,000	1,042
Whitehorse	South Dakota	2007	1,100	1,169
Strohm	Oklahoma	2008	1,000	713
Total			**22,100**	**22,101**

Source: BLM.

Similarly, the number of long-term holding facilities has increased, as has the cost. The number of facilities increased from 1 in 1988 to 11 as of June 2008, and the number of animals cared for increased from 1,500 in 2000 to 22,101 as of June 2008 (see table 11). These long-term holding facilities have reached their capacity—currently 22,100—despite the increase in numbers of facilities. BLM anticipates it will need greater long-term holding capacity and is working to contract for additional facilities.

BLM pays private contractors an average of $1.27 per horse per day to maintain the animals for the remainder of their lifespan, unless removed from long-term holding for adoption or sale. While this fee has increased by only 7 cents since 2000, the number of animals cared for has also increased, resulting in a significant increase in BLM spending on long-term holding.[41] In 2000, BLM spent approximately $668,000 in 2000, compared to more than $9.1 million in 2007 to care for wild horses in long-term holding. The long-term holding facilities are primarily located in Oklahoma and Kansas, where forage is typically more abundant than on HMAs of the West. Table 12 lists the 11 long-term holding facilities.

For at least two decades, BLM's primary strategy to manage excess unadoptable wild horses has been to increase long-term holding, despite warnings in our 1990 report that these facilities were likely to be more expensive than envisioned and to be only a temporary solution to the disposal of unadoptable animals.[42] In 1994, the Department of the Interior's Office of Inspector General also issued a report that strongly discouraged long-term holding as a solution to managing horses removed from the range due to the large costs.[43] BLM continues to look for more facilities but faces difficulty attracting new contractors that can sustain a large number of animals and that will accept the fee BLM offers, compared to perhaps more profitable land uses.

BLM Has Controls in Place to Help Ensure the Humane Treatment of Wild Horses and Burros, but It Could Better Track and Report these Data to the Public

BLM has implemented multiple controls to help ensure the humane treatment of wild horses and burros, including standard operating procedures and agreements with all three slaughterhouses in the United States before they closed in 2007. A variety of controls are used at various stages in the management of wild horses and burros, including for those animals that are gathered, in short-term holding facilities, in long-term holding facilities, adopted, or sold. BLM's controls for gathers include standard operating procedures, inspections, and data collection. While BLM state offices collect detailed data on animals that die during gathers, the information is not compiled by BLM headquarters in its centralized database, nor is it reported to the public. In addition, BLM does not regularly provide the information it tracks on the treatment of animals in short- and long-term holding and adoption inspections to the public. Making more of this data available to the public may help inform them about the treatment of the animals and improve transparency. Beginning in 1998, until the last horse slaughterhouse in the United States shut down in 2007, BLM sought agreements with all three slaughter facilities to alert BLM of wild horses that entered their facilities. According to BLM data, since 2002, about 2,000 wild horses whose legal titles were obtained by private citizens either through adoption or purchase were slaughtered. During that same period, another 90 wild horses whose title still belonged to BLM were retrieved from slaughterhouses by BLM and by wild horse groups. We reviewed the basic controls BLM has in place, but we did not evaluate their effectiveness. While BLM is required to implement controls to help ensure the humane treatment of wild horses and burros, such be met.[44]

BLM Internal Controls Help Ensure Humane Treatment, but BLM Could Improve Data Gathering and Reporting in some Areas

A variety of controls are used at various stages in the management of wild horses and burros, including for those animals that are gathered, in short-term holding facilities, in long-term holding facilities, adopted, or sold. BLM's controls for gathers include standard operating procedures, inspections, and data collection. Data collected from 6 of the 10 states from fiscal years 2005 through 2007 indicate that mortality as a result of gathers is about 1.2 percent. Similarly, controls for short- and long-term holding include standard operating procedures, inspections, and data collection. BLM did not report any deaths due to neglect or abuse at holding facilities, aside from one animal that was repossessed by BLM after having been abused by an adopter. BLM has controls over the adoption of wild horses and burros, and data indicate that from 2005 to 2007, about 9 percent of adopters were not in compliance with BLM's standards of care. BLM's controls over humane treatment primarily apply to horses and burros before ownership is passed to private individuals, but BLM has also implemented some controls to protect horses and burros once ownership passes, such as when wild horses and burros are sold. For animals that are sold, since spring 2005, BLM has required buyers to sign a statement that they do not intend to slaughter the animals. BLM does not consistently track information on treatment during gather operations through a central database, nor does it report information about the treatment of animals during gathers, holding, or adoption inspections to the public.

Source: BLM.

Figure 8. Helicopter Used to Gather Wild Horses Near Ely, Nevada, c. 2006.

Gathers

BLM has established controls, such as standard operating procedures and tracking systems, to help ensure humane treatment during gather operations. BLM hires contractors to remove wild horses and burros from the range. These contractors generally use helicopters to herd the animals into capture pens on the range (see Figure 8).

Due to the stress caused to wild animals by gathering them into pens, gather operations have the potential to cause harm to wild horses and burros, such as nervous agitation; conflict between captured animals; or more rarely, animal death. Because of the potential for harm and to help ensure the safe and humane handling of all animals captured, BLM has implemented a range of standard operating procedures for its gather contractors. Prior to the start of gather operations, BLM personnel evaluate the site of the gather to determine whether it is suitable based on environmental and safety concerns. They also approve gather facility plans ensuring, among other things, that they do not present puncture or laceration hazards and that they prevent animals from seeing humans, vehicles, and other perceived threats. During the herding of the animals, BLM sets limitations on the distance and speed the animals will travel, depending on the condition of the animals and other factors. As the animals are herded into the gather site, BLM requires contractors to segregate horses by age and sex to reduce the possibility of conflict and to ensure that very young horses and burros are not left behind to fend for themselves on the range. Finally, as the captured animals are transported from the gather site to short-term holding facilities, contractors are required to follow procedures to ensure animal safety, such as using adequately sized motorized equipment that has been inspected for safety. BLM has managed gathers with standard operating procedures since the passage of the act in 1971.

Although BLM's controls are designed to enhance the safety of wild horses and burros during gather operations, some animals are accidentally killed in the course of gathers or are euthanized because of ill health or prior injury. Six of the 10 BLM state offices reported data about the number of animals that die as a result of their gather operations. Data collected from 6 of the 10 states from fiscal years 2005 through 2007 indicate that, of the 24,855 animals removed from these states during this period, about 1.2 percent were either euthanized or died accidentally (see table 13). Horses and burros sometimes die due to accidents during gather operations on the range or after they are brought to the holding pens. For example, wild horses will sometimes panic and break their necks against capture pens. Animals found with conditions that make it unlikely they will be able to live their life without significant pain, such as lameness or club feet, are euthanized.

Although BLM national and state officials told us that they sometimes record data about the animals accidentally killed or euthanized during gathers at the BLM state office level, BLM does not centrally compile or report these data to the public on a regular basis on a national level. A BLM official told us that although their main tracking database has the capability to record the number of animals that are killed or euthanized during gathers, they generally do not use the database to do so because it was originally intended to track adoptions. Moreover, BLM has not regularly reported to the public how many wild horses and burros are killed in the course of gathers, although BLM officials have cited the data during public hearings. Some advocates and members of the public believe that gathers are held in secret and highlight individual cases of apparent mistreatment as evidence that inhumane treatment is widespread.

Table 13. Number and Percentage of Wild Horses and Burros That Died During Gather Operations, (for 6 of 10 States) Fiscal Years 2005 through 2007

Fiscal year	Number removed	Number of accidental deaths	Percentage	Number euthanized	Percentage
2005	9,830	25	0.25%	46	0.47%
2006	8,081	64	0.79	79	0.98
2007	6,944	28	0.40	60	0.86
Total	**24,855**	**117**	**0.47%**	**185**	**0.74%**

Source: GAO analysis of BLM data.

Note: This chart is based on data reported by 6 of 10 states: California, Colorado, Idaho, Nevada, New Mexico, and Wyoming. The data provided could not be verified for its reliability. We requested this information from the other four states (Arizona, Montana, Oregon, and Utah), but the information was not provided.

However, a BLM official told us that it is BLM's standard practice to allow the public and the media to observe gather operations, and BLM is required to hold public hearings prior to scheduled gathers using helicopters. If BLM does not improve its transparency by presenting reliable data to members of the public, BLM will continue to be vulnerable to accusations that gathers are generally cruel and inhumane.

Source: GAO.

Figure 9. BLM Contractor Trimming Horse Hooves Using a Special Holding Chute at a Contract Short-Term Holding Facility in Fallon, Nevada, October 2007.

Short-Term Holding

BLM has issued standard operating procedures to help ensure that wild horses and burros held in short-term holding facilities are well cared for. They include procedures for minimizing the excitement of the animals to prevent injury; separating horses by age, sex, and size; observation of the animals on a regular basis; and recording information about the animals that BLM later uses for tracking the animals in BLM's database. BLM's short-term holding facilities are mostly maintained and directly managed by BLM, either on government property or on leased property. Several are at state prisons, and a few others are maintained by contractors in privately-owned feedlots or ranches that BLM has leased. According to BLM staff, they regularly inspect the short-term holding facilities and the animals they hold. They inspect to see that the corral equipment is up to code and that animals are treated with appropriate veterinary care. For example, staff check to see that the horses' hooves are regularly trimmed so that they do not become too long and cause injury. At two of the short-term holding facilities we visited, we observed specially constructed chutes that hold and rotate horses in place so that horses' hooves can be trimmed more quickly, easily, and with less risk to the animals and the employee than other methods, such as using tranquilizer darts or roping (see Figure 9).

BLM data indicate that the wild horses and burros held in short-term holding facilities from 2003 to 2007 had a mortality rate of about 5 percent. Specifically, for 2007, BLM reported 936 deaths in short-term holding facilities out of a total of 17,363 animals that passed through short-term holding facilities in that year.[45] BLM reported that none of the animals in its care died of neglect or abuse between 2005 and 2007, aside from one case in 2006, where a reclaimed adopted horse died in BLM care due to the effects of abuse suffered while it was in the care of an adopter. BLM data showed that the animals generally died due to sickness, broken limbs, or injuries sustained accidentally during gathers. BLM does not report this information regularly to members of the public who remain concerned that the agency does not adequately care for animals in short-term holding.

Long-Term Holding

BLM has similar controls in place for its long-term holding facilities. BLM staff inspect long-term holding facilities annually to count the number of animals held. Staff also monitor pasture conditions, winter feeding, and animal health throughout the year. According to BLM staff, during these visits they ensure the contractors comply with BLM provisions and discuss possible problems that can be corrected. In addition, veterinary staff from the Department of Agriculture's Animal and Plant Health Inspection Service inspect long-term holding facilities annually; these inspections involve a full count of the horses held there, an inspection of the horses' general health, and written reports. Animal and Plant Health Inspection Service reports from 2007 indicate that the horses kept in long-term holding sanctuaries are generally in "good" or "excellent" condition. These reports, however, highlight some areas for possible improvement. At one facility, one area of improvement included the proper disposal of the remains of animals that have died of natural causes. To help ensure the animals are well cared for, a contract veterinarian provides care when needed at BLM direction and expense. In addition to inspecting the facilities for the well being of wild horses in long-term holding, contractors are required to count and report the number of horses held on a weekly basis for billing and payment purposes. In 2007, long-term holding contractors were paid an average fee of $1.27 per horse per day, or about $460 per horse per year. While this contract fee structure is not in itself a control that guarantees humane treatment, it provides a profit incentive for contractors to ensure the continued health of the horses. According to one BLM official, BLM does not regularly document the results of its inspections. This official told us that the agency would take actions and record them if it found problems, but the official generally has not found problems with the contractors that have warranted action beyond informal conversations to address minor issues.

BLM collects data on how wild horses are cared for in long-term holding, including the number of animals that die in long-term holding. The average mortality rate of wild horses in long-term holding from 2003 through 2007 was about 8 percent, but it fluctuated from a low of 5 percent to a high of 14 percent during that time period. Specifically, for 2007, BLM reported 938 deaths in long-term holding facilities.[46] The number of wild horses in long-term holding in 2007 was 19,652. The animals that die in long-term holding are generally found in the pastures, and unless there is evidence of foul play, BLM does not investigate the cause of death. According to BLM, barring any evidence to the contrary, it is assumed that the animals in long-term holding die of old age. Officially, BLM reported about 95 percent of the animal deaths in long-term holding as "undiagnosed." Some of the other causes of deaths reported included old age and respiratory illness. No animals in long-term holding died from neglect or abuse, according to BLM reports. While BLM collects this data, it does not report this data regularly to the public. In the absence of this data, some members of the public who advocate greater protection for wild horses have repeatedly expressed their concern that BLM does not adequately care for animals in long-term holding.

Adoption

The act requires BLM to determine that adopters have provided humane conditions, treatment, and care for adopted animals for at least 1 year before BLM transfers ownership to the adopter. To implement the act, BLM has established policies for inspecting adopted horses or burros in this first year through telephone calls or personal visits. BLM inspections focus on the condition of the animal; the condition of the facilities; and whether the adopter has notified BLM if the adopted animal has been moved, was stolen, has escaped, or has died. Prior to taking possession of an adopted animal, BLM requires that adopters describe the facility where they will maintain the adopted animal. This is documented in their application, which confers penalties for providing false information.

According to BLM data, from 2005 through 2007, an average of about 9 percent of adopted wild horses and burros that still belong to the government have not been treated in compliance with BLM standards (see table 14). BLM randomly selects a sample from the universe of approximately 5,000 adopters per year who have not yet received title of their adopted animal for inspection. BLM inspects these adopters in order to generate a statistical sample of the likely percentage of adopted animals kept under conditions that do not comply with BLM's policies and standards. The most common conditions in need of improvement included the failure to report changes in the animal's location or status and substandard facilities, such as inadequate fencing or shelter. Less common conditions included lack of care of the animal, such as inadequate feeding or failure to trim the animal's hooves before they grew too long.

Table 14. Results of Random Inspections of Wild Horse and Burro Adoptions, 2005 through 2007

Result of random adoption inspections	2005		2006		2007	
	Number	Percent	Number	Percent	Number	Percent
No violation	395	94%	614	91%	805	89%
Failure to notify BLM of change in status	10	2	24	4	36	4
Failure to provide adequate facilities/care	4	1	3	0	30	3
Failure to produce animal	5	1	13	2	19	2
Unauthorized transfer/sale	0	0	6	1	15	2
Commercial exploitation	0	0	0	0	4	0
Inadequate facility	4	1	6	1	0	0
Unauthorized destruction	0	0	5	1	0	0
Inhumane treatment	2	0	0	0	0	0
Total	**420**	**100%**	**671**	**100%**	**909**	**100%**

Source: GAO analysis of BLM data.

In addition, BLM policy directs that officials or certified volunteers conduct personal inspections of all adopted animals whenever BLM receives complaints about mistreatment or when an individual or organization adopts more than four wild horses or burros at one time.

Similar to the data collected on the animals in short- and long-term holding, BLM does not provide information on the results of its adoption inspections to the public. The information regularly provided to the public on the treatment of these animals is in contrast to the comparatively large amount of information BLM provides on the program's Web site regarding information on AML and population estimates for each HMA.

Sales

In the case of animals that were legally sold, BLM has implemented limitations to prevent these animals from being resold to slaughter facilities. In 2004, the act was changed and directed BLM to sell, "without limitation," excess wild horses and burros more than 10 years of age or that had been offered unsuccessfully for adoption at least three times, until all excess animals for sale are sold or until AML is met in all HMAs. However, shortly after BLM began to sell wild horses and burros without limitation, in early 2005, it was discovered that 41 of these wild horses had been slaughtered. In April 2005, BLM suspended its wild horse sales program and resumed sales in May 2005, after adding controls intended to restrict the sale of animals for the purpose of selling them for slaughter. These controls included BLM's requirement that buyers sign a statement they do not intend to sell the animals for slaughter and verification that potential buyers would provide adequate care for the animals.

BLM Implemented Controls to Prevent Slaughter of Wild Horses in the United States

Although BLM is no longer required to protect animals after ownership has passed to adopters or buyers, BLM implemented controls to help prevent their slaughter beginning in 1998. BLM had negotiated agreements with all three U.S. facilities that operated horse slaughterhouses. The slaughterhouses agreed to alert BLM to all wild horses that entered their facilities and refrain from slaughtering those wild horses whose title still belonged to BLM. According to BLM data, which it was able to provide since 2002, about 2,000 wild horses whose legal titles were obtained by private citizens through adoption or purchase were slaughtered. During that same time period, at least 90 adopted wild horses that were still owned by the government were brought to these slaughterhouses, and all were retrieved by BLM and interested wild horse groups.

As of fall 2007, all horse slaughter facilities in the United States had been shut down following unsuccessful legal challenges to state laws effectively banning the practice. In January 2007, the U.S. Court of Appeals for the Fifth Circuit ruled that a 1949 Texas law banning the sale, possession, or transfer of horsemeat applied to the two slaughterhouses in Texas.[47] In September 2007, the U.S. Court of Appeals for the Seventh Circuit upheld an Illinois ban.[48] These rulings effectively closed the plants and ended horse slaughter in the United States.

Even though all horse slaughter facilities in the United States have been closed, it is still possible for wild horses and burros to be sold to facilities outside the United States.[49] Prior to the closure of all U.S. horse slaughter facilities, about 50,000 domestic horses were brought to slaughter in the United States annually between 2001 and 2004. Generally, exporting horses and burros to other countries for slaughter, such as Canada or Mexico, is not prohibited; for example, about 3,000 horses per month were exported for slaughter in 2007, according to Department of Agriculture information. We attempted to determine how many of these horses were at one time wild, but we were not able to do so. The Department of Agriculture, which certifies the inspections of horses and other livestock exported to other countries, is not required and does not report how many of the horses exported to other countries were once wild horses.

Challenges to the Long-Term Sustainability of the Program Include Growing Holding Costs and Limited Options for Dealing with Unadoptable Animals

The long-term sustainability of BLM's Wild Horse and Burro Program depends on the resolution of two significant challenges. First, holding costs are overwhelming the program's ability to manage animals on the range and will continue to do so if BLM does not consider alternatives to holding. Second, BLM has limited options for dealing with unadoptable animals off of the range because its alternatives under the act—humane destruction of the animals or selling the animals without limitation—are thought to be unacceptable to the public. As a result, BLM has placed over 30,000 wild horses and burros in holding.

If not Controlled, Off-the-range Holding Costs will Continue to Overwhelm the Program

The portion of the Wild Horse and Burro Program's spending that is directed toward short- and long-term holding has increased from 46 percent of the program's direct costs in 2000 to 67 percent in 2007. This increase leaves a smaller portion of the budget available for on-the-range management activities. Much of the increase has occurred because accelerated removals implemented to reach AML have coincided with a decline in adoption demand. Because long-term holding facilities are at capacity, BLM has had little choice but to hold excess unadoptable horses in more expensive short-term holding. BLM's spending on short- and long-term holding has increased from about $7.0 million in 2000, or 46 percent of the program's direct costs, to about $20.9 million in 2007, or 67 percent of the program's direct costs (see Figure 10). In 2008, BLM anticipates that holding costs will account for about 74 percent of the program's direct costs. To deal with its long-term holding problem, BLM has primarily sought increased funding to open additional long-term holding facilities. However, funding is not likely to increase in the future, and limited funding is forcing BLM to make difficult choices. For example, in January 2008, BLM considered canceling all remaining removals scheduled for the fiscal year because of the amount needed for short- and long-term holding. As of July 2008, BLM was seeking the funds to continue these removals by redirecting money from other BLM activities to the Wild Horse and Burro Program. As a result, under current funding levels, BLM must now choose between either managing the range to prevent overpopulation or exercise one or both of its other options—destroying animals or selling them without limitation.

To continue to reduce overpopulation on the range by using gathers alone, BLM projects that the program's budget would have to increase to about $77 million by fiscal year 2012, from about $36 million in 2008. If BLM does not receive this increase or exercise its other options to reduce populations off the range, then it will not have sufficient funds to manage wild horses and burros on the range, and populations will sharply increase. BLM's current projections indicate that caring for unadoptable animals would reduce the agency's ability to gather horses to an average of about 4,500 animals per year, which would only be enough to prevent animals from dying from the effects of overpopulation and drought. At these removal levels, BLM projects that the on-the-range population would reach 50,000 animals by 2012—about 80 percent greater than the upper limit of AML. This on-the-range population level would be greater than the population level prior to the beginning of BLM's 2001 strategic plan.

Since 2004, BLM has had the goal of reducing the total population on the range to the midpoint of AML. If it were to reach this level, which is currently about 22,588 animals, an annual population growth rate of 20 percent would require the annual removal of about 4,500 animals to maintain that level, approximately equal to the recent adoption rate. Assuming that rate remained constant, fewer animals would be sent to long-term holding. However, even if BLM is able to reach a balance between animals removed and those adopted, it still has the challenge of dealing with 30,088 animals that are currently held in short-term and long-term holding facilities across the country. Furthermore the number of animals held in holding would exceed 40,000 animals if BLM were to remove the approximately 11,000 animals necessary to reach the midpoint of AML.

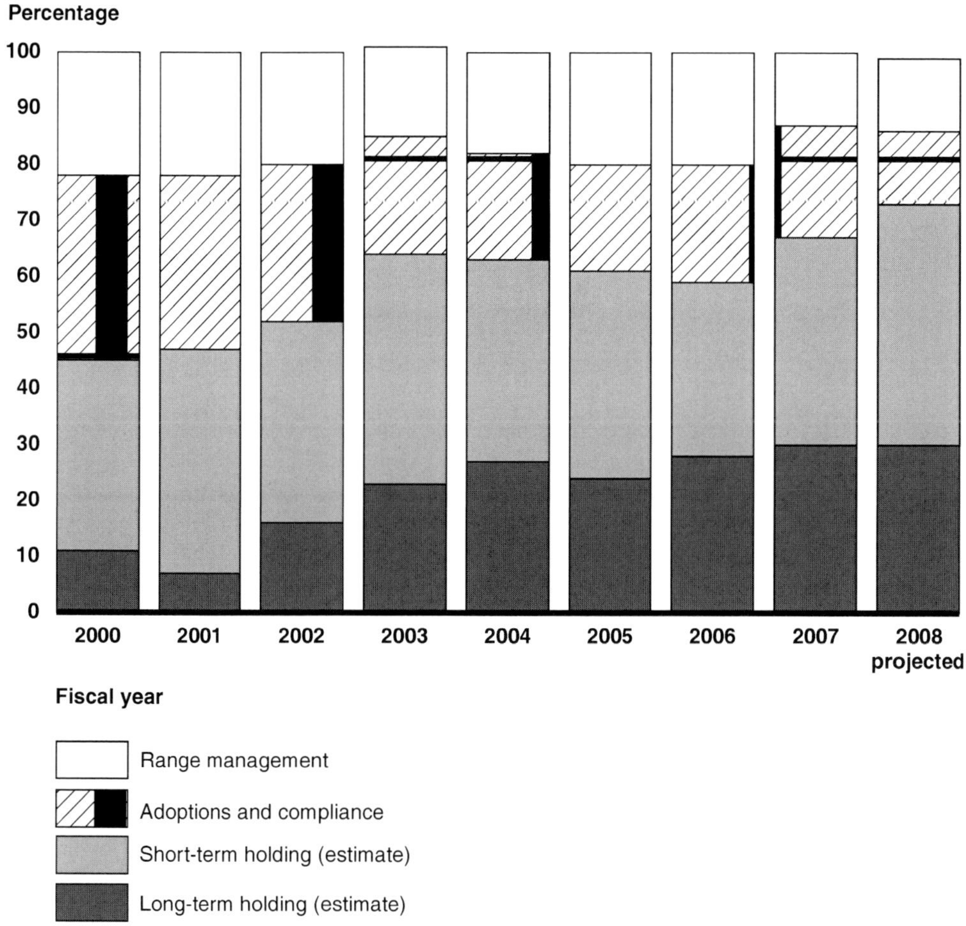

Source: GAO analysis of BLM data.

Note: This chart represents direct program spending. It omits spending on overhead items—which average about $7 million per year—such as administrative costs, vehicle costs, and other nondirect program related costs.

Figure 10. BLM Estimated Wild Horse and Burro Direct Program Costs, Fiscal Years 2000 through 2008.

BLM has a number of research projects under way and ideas in development that could slow the increase in the population on the range. These include fertility control efforts, such as the development of a fertility vaccine (see app. II for more information on this vaccine) and releasing sterilized male horses back to the range after capture. Given that many existing HMAs are already over AML, releasing a large number of sterilized male horses or nonreproducing herds back to the range as a means of trying to reduce future holding costs would likely require changing existing land use decisions within BLM's existing authority to increase AMLs, expand existing HMAs or designate new HMAs; or through seeking new legislative authority. Under the 1971 act, the land available for the management of wild horses and burros is limited to the areas where they existed at the time of the act. The originally designated herd areas consisted of 53.5 million acres compared to the existing

HMA acreage of 34.3 million, a difference of 19.2 million acres. Specifically, the BLM owned acreage managed for wild horses and burros has changed from 42.2 million acres to 29.0 million acres, a difference of 13.2 million acres. As we mentioned earlier, BLM is in the process of compiling a history of actions that led to these changes. At this point, however, it is not clear how much of the 13.2 million acres is still public land under BLM's control.

While BLM could change AMLs, expand existing HMAs, or designate new HMAs within its existing authority, BLM is a multiple use agency and it weighs the needs of wild horses and burros against other competing uses. Alternatively, should BLM chose to do so, new legislative authority could be pursued to allow nonreproducing herds to be relocated to areas where they were not found at the time of the act. We believe that it is important to consider increasing AML or expanding HMA acreage only as a means to accommodate nonreproducing herds. Increasing the number of reproducing animals on the range without corresponding solutions for fertility control or declining adoption demand will, in the long run, only exacerbate BLM's problems with dealing with excess animals.

Under Current Law BLM's Options are Limited for Dealing with Unadoptable Animals

Despite these budget problems, BLM has avoided using two options in the act for dealing with unadoptable animals because of concerns over the public and congressional reaction to the large-scale slaughter of thousands of healthy horses. The Wild Free-Roaming Horses and Burros Act, as amended, requires that excess animals, for which the adoption demand is not sufficient to absorb all the animals removed from the range, be destroyed in the most humane and cost-efficient manner possible or, under certain circumstances, be sold without limitation. The 1978 amendments to the original 1971 act directed that "[t]he Secretary shall cause additional excess wild free-roaming horses and burros for which an adoption demand by qualified individuals does not exist to be destroyed in the most humane and cost efficient manner possible."[50] From 1981 to 1982, BLM destroyed at least 47 excess animals. BLM decided not to destroy excess unadoptable animals in 1982 after the Director issued a policy prohibiting the destruction of healthy animals because of public dismay. Furthermore, from fiscal year 1988 through fiscal year 2004, Congress prohibited BLM from using its Management of Lands and Resources appropriations to destroy excess healthy, unadoptable wild horses and burros.

In our 1990 report, we found that keeping excess animals in long-term holding was costly and recommended that BLM examine alternatives, such as sterilizing animals and releasing them back into the wild.[51] Although BLM was prohibited from using its Management of Lands and Resources appropriations for humanely destroying excess animals through consider this action as a last resort in the event that Congress lifted the prohibition in the future. The recurring prohibition in the annual appropriations bills ended after fiscal year 2004. Since then, BLM has no longer been prohibited from using its Management of Lands and Resources appropriations for carrying out the requirement to destroy excess animals. BLM still has not used this option.

In 2004, Congress provided BLM with an alternative to destroying unadoptable excess animals by amending the act to state that "[a]ny excess animal or the remains of an excess animal shall be sold if—(A) the excess animal is more than 10 years of age; or (B) the excess animal has been offered unsuccessfully for adoption at least 3 times."[52] Furthermore, the amendment stipulated that the excess animals "shall be made available for sale without limitation."[53] BLM has instead imposed limitations on the sales of excess animals in an effort to reduce the risk that animals purchased at a low price would be resold to slaughterhouses for profit.

As a result, BLM is not in compliance with the act. BLM officials told us that they have chosen not to destroy excess animals or sell them without limitation because of concerns about public and congressional reaction to the large-scale slaughter of thousands of healthy horses. Various BLM officials at different levels of responsibility also told us that the agency has not complied with these provisions because doing so would cause an immediate threat to the careers of any officials involved, due to the anticipated negative reaction of the public and Congress. Nevertheless, as of June 2008, budget constraints forced BLM to reconsider all of its options, officials told us. Specifically, for fiscal year 2009, BLM is considering euthanizing about 2,300 horses from short-term holding—about one-third of the animals currently in short-term holding. In addition, they are considering selling without limitation about 8,000 animals from both short- and long-term holding. However, as of August 31, 2008, legislation was pending in the 110th Congress that would repeal the directive for BLM to sell animals without limitation, but not the requirement to destroy unadoptable excess horses.[54]

Other than one pilot project, BLM has not initiated strategies to reduce the number of horses they currently manage in long-term holding and has not formally considered other possible solutions to indefinitely caring for horses in long-term holding. BLM officials who lead state Wild Horse and Burro Programs suggested several actions that could be taken to alleviate off-the-range costs to the program, but many of these changes would require changes in the law or BLM regulations. The most common suggestion, made by 4 of the 10 state leads, was that the federal government should provide incentives for private individuals or organizations to care for unwanted wild horses, such as monetary incentives or tax deductions. In 2003, BLM initiated a pilot project in Wyoming to pay private ranchers a one-time lump sum to care for unadoptable excess animals. This pilot project ended because of a lack of up-front funds. In addition, a BLM official familiar with the project told us that private ranchers had less interest in the project as the market for cattle grazing improved. Implementing tax deductions would likely require changes in the tax law. Another suggestion made by three of the state leads was that the act should be changed to allow the government to manage unadoptable wild horses and burros on public or private lands outside areas where they were originally found. The act currently does not allow BLM to relocate wild horses and burros to areas of public lands where they were not found when the act was passed. To date, BLM has not sought the legislative changes that would make these suggestions possible.

CONCLUSIONS

The management of a program consisting of wild free-roaming animals is unique within BLM, and it presents distinct management challenges. While BLM has made significant progress in increasing the number of HMAs that have set AML and in moving toward meeting AML, its recent removal efforts have resulted in the agency managing almost the same number of animals off of the range as they manage in the wild. By spending an ever increasing amount of funding on caring for animals off the range, little funding is left to conduct important on-the-range management activities, as originally envisioned in the act. Now that BLM is closer to meeting AML, it is important for field offices to have the resources necessary to maintain those levels and to monitor whether those levels indeed create the "thriving natural ecological balance" called for in the act.

Future changes to AML determinations should be based on consistent factors across HMAs. With the turnover of the more experienced senior BLM staff that set the existing AMLs to newer more junior staff, it is important that the newer staff have clear official guidance to follow on making AML determinations. It is also important for the management of the program that BLM have the most accurate population estimates possible. While counting wild free-roaming animals is an inherently challenging task, the widespread use of statistically based counting methods across more HMAs, as appropriate, would provide a scientifically sound basis for compensating for possible undercounts. BLM provides a great deal of information about the Wild Horse and Burro Program through its Web site, including information on AML and population estimates for each HMA. However, despite public concerns about the humane treatment of these animals, BLM has not provided the public with easily accessible information about their treatment. In some cases, BLM headquarters does not centrally compile information on the treatment of animals during gathers. Providing the public with additional information on the treatment of animals during gathers and once they are removed from the range would help inform the public about their treatment.

In our 1990 report, we noted that given the amount of federal resources needed to maintain unadoptable excess horses in long-term holding, BLM would need to seek alternative options. At the time, we recommended that BLM consider a variety of disposal options for these horses that were not being used, including sterilization and euthanasia. Today, about 20 years after the first long-term holding facility opened, with adoption demand declining and alternative disposal options still not being used, BLM is continuing to open new long-term holding facilities to care for unadoptable wild horses, and the costs continue to escalate. Cost-effective alternatives for long-term holding are still needed.

BLM is faced with a dilemma as it attempts to comply with the act. On one hand, the act directs BLM to protect and preserve wild horses and burros, and on the other hand the act directs BLM to destroy excess animals for which an adoption demand does not exist or, under certain circumstances, to sell them without limitation, which has led to the slaughter of some animals. BLM has committed to caring for these animals, even though the law requires their humane destruction or sale without limitation and the cost for their care off-the-range is now overwhelming the program. The program is at a critical crossroads. Within the program's existing budget, BLM cannot afford to care for all of the animals off the range, while at the same time managing wild horse and burro populations on the range. Resource limitations are forcing BLM to reconsider all available management options, and a workable solution must be developed to bring BLM into compliance with the act.

Recommendations for Executive Action

We make five recommendations to the Secretary of the Interior.

To improve the management of BLM's Wild Horse and Burro Program, we make four recommendations that the Secretary of the Interior direct BLM to:

- finalize and issue the new *Wild Horse and Burro Program Handbook* that establishes a policy for setting AML to ensure that AML is determined based on consistent factors across HMAs into the future;
- continue to adopt and employ statistically based methods to estimate animal populations across HMAs, such as those being evaluated by animal population researchers, to improve the accuracy of population estimates integral to BLM's management of wild horses and burros on the range and in planning for capacity needed for excess animals once they are removed from the range;
- track the number of animals harmed or killed during the gather process in a centralized database system and determine what information on the treatment of gathered animals, short-term and long-term holding animals, and adopted animals could easily be provided to the public to help inform them about the treatment of wild horses and burros; and
- develop cost-effective alternatives to the process of caring for wild horses removed from the range in long-term holding facilities and seek the legislative changes that may be necessary to implement those alternatives.

To address BLM's noncompliance with the act, as amended, we recommend that the Secretary of the Interior direct BLM to discuss with Congress and other stakeholders how best to comply with the act or amend it so that BLM would be able to comply. As part of this discussion, BLM should inform Congress of its concerns with (1) the act's requirement for the humane destruction of excess animals and (2) the possible slaughter of healthy horses if excess animals are sold without limitation, under certain circumstances, as the act requires.

Agency Comments and Our Evaluation

We provided a draft of this report to the Department of the Interior for review and comment. The department concurred with our findings and recommendations and believes they will help to improve the Wild Horse and Burro Program. In addition, the department provided several technical clarifications, which we incorporated as appropriate. Appendix IV contains the Department of the Interior's comment letter.

As agreed with your office, unless you publicly announce the contents of this report earlier, we plan no further distribution until 30 days from the report date. At that time, we will send copies of this report to the Secretary of the Interior, the Director of BLM, and other interested parties. We will also make copies available to others upon request. In addition, the report will be available at no charge on the GAO Web site at http://www.gao.gov.

If you or your staff has any questions about this report, please contact me at (202) 512-3841 or nazzaror@gao.gov. Contact points for our Offices of Congressional Relations and

Public Affairs may be found on the last page of this report. GAO staff who made major contributions to this report are listed in appendix V.

Sincerely yours,

Robin M. Nazzaro
Director,
Natural Resources and Environment

Appendix I: Objectives, Scope, and Methodology

We examined (1) the Bureau of Land Management's (BLM) progress in managing wild horses and burros on the range through setting and meeting appropriate management levels (AML); (2) BLM's management of wild horses and burros off of the range through adoption, sales, and holding facilities; (3) the controls BLM has in place to help ensure humane treatment of wild horses and burros; and (4) what challenges, if any, BLM faces in managing for the long-term sustainability of the Wild Horse and Burro Program. We were also asked to review how and why the acreage available for wild horses and burros had changed since the 1971 act. We did not examine the acreage issue because BLM is in the process of compiling a history of acreage determinations. BLM officials expect their review to be completed by March 2009.

To examine how BLM manages wild horses and burros on and off of the range and to identify the challenges facing BLM, we reviewed relevant laws, regulations, BLM policy, and BLM strategic plans. We also surveyed, and analyzed documents from, 26 of the 44 BLM field offices that manage wild horses and burros.[1] We collected and reviewed relevant resource management decision documents from the surveyed field offices to help corroborate their responses about specific questions, including those about factors used to make AML determinations and gather decisions. We surveyed field offices in all 10 western states that manage HMAs. The field offices we surveyed represent 82 percent of all BLM acres managed for wild horses and burros, 74 percent of all BLM managed wild horses, and 69 percent of burros on the range at the time of the survey. Our survey sample included 100 percent of the BLM field offices that manage HMAs in Nevada, including the Tonopah Field Station (seven offices); three randomly selected field offices from each of the five states whose field offices or district offices manage a population of wild horses and burros that fall between 1,000 and 10,000 horses (Arizona, California, Oregon, Utah, and Wyoming); and one randomly selected field office from each of the four states whose field offices manage a population of wild horses and burros that is less than 1,000 (Colorado, Idaho, Montana, and New Mexico). Because most of our survey questions focused on the management of a particular HMA, we judgmentally selected an HMA for each field office to consider in responding to our survey. We considered a variety of factors in making these HMA

[1] We drew our sample of 26 field units from among the 44 field units that manage Herd Management Areas (HMA), which include 39 field offices, 4 district offices in Oregon, and 1 field station in Nevada. We will refer to these 44 BLM field units collectively as field offices. BLM's count of the number of offices that manage HMAs may differ because the 4 district offices in Oregon manage 7 resource area offices.

selections, including herd population size and whether the HMA had met or not met AML (according to 2007 BLM Statistics). Table 15 lists the 26 BLM field offices and HMAs we selected as part of our survey.

Table 15. BLM Field Offices and HMAs Included in GAO's Survey

BLM field office by state	HMA
Arizona	
Yuma Field Office	Cibola–Trigo
Hassayampa Field Office	Lake Pleasant
Kingman Field Office	Black Mountain
California	
Surprise Field Office	High Rock
Alturas Field Office	Red Rock Lakes
Ridgecrest Field Office	Centennial
Colorado	
White River Field Office	Piceance–East Douglas Creek
Idaho	
Four Rivers Field Office	Four Mile
Montana	
Billings Field Office	Pryor Mountain Wild Horse Range
Nevada	
Tonopah Field Station	Montezuma Peak
Battle Mountain Field Office	South Shoshone
Carson City Field Office	Flanigan
Elko Field Office	Rock Creek
Ely Field Office	Dry Lake
Las Vegas Field Office	Red Rock
Winnimucca Field Office	Granite Range
New Mexico	
Socorro Field Office	Bordo Atravesado
Oregon	
Prineville District Office	Liggett Table
Lakeview District Office	Beaty's Butte
Vale District Office	Coyote Lake–Alvord Tule Springs
Utah	
Richfield Field Office	Canyon Lands
Vernal Field Office	Hill Creek
Fillmore Field Office	Conger
Wyoming	
Rock Springs Field Office	Divide Basin
Cody Field Office	McCullough Peaks
Lander Field Office	Dishpan Butte

Source: GAO.

The survey included several open-ended responses aimed at determining the primary challenges associated with meeting and maintaining AML, the primary challenges facing the Wild Horse and Burro Program as a whole, and suggestions for ways to improve the program. Two GAO analysts independently reviewed these open-ended survey responses, agreed upon the categories for coding each response, and resolved any disagreements in coding to determine what the respondents as a whole thought about these issues.

The practical difficulties of conducting any survey may introduce errors, commonly referred to as nonsampling errors. For example, difficulties in how a particular question is interpreted, in the sources of information that are available to the respondents, or in how the data are entered into a database or were analyzed can introduce unwanted variability into the survey results. We took steps in the development of the questionnaire, the data collection, and the data analysis to minimize these nonsampling errors. For example, survey specialists designed the questionnaire in collaboration with GAO staff with subject matter expertise. Then, the draft questionnaire was pretested with officials from five BLM field offices in four different states to ensure that the questions were relevant, clearly stated, and easy to comprehend. We also conducted follow-up phone calls to clarify ambiguous or incomplete responses. We received usable responses from all field offices that we surveyed—a 100 percent response rate. See appendix III for a summary of the survey responses not presented elsewhere in the report.

We also interviewed agency officials at BLM Headquarters; the National Program Office in Reno, Nevada; and Wild Horse and Burro Program State Leads from each of the 10 states that manage wild horses and burros. In addition, we conducted site visits at two field offices that manage HMAs in Nevada and Colorado; one long-term holding facility in Oklahoma; three short-term holding facilities in Colorado, Nevada, and Wyoming; and attended two adoption events in Arizona and Colorado.

To examine humane treatment, we reviewed relevant laws, regulations, and BLM policies. We collected and analyzed reports from BLM Headquarters, state offices, and data from BLM's compliance database. We also interviewed BLM compliance officials from two states, a veterinarian from the Department of Agriculture's Animal and Plant Health Inspection Service, and public citizens and advocacy groups that work to promote the well being of wild horses and burros.

As part of our overall methodology, we interviewed a range of stakeholders interested in BLM's management of the Wild Horse and Burro Program, including, but not limited to, the American Wild Horse Preservation Campaign, the Animal Welfare Institute, the Cloud Foundation, the Humane Society of the United States, the National Cattlemen's Beef Association, and Nevada Bighorns Unlimited.

We conducted this performance audit from September 2007 to October 2008 in accordance with generally accepted government auditing standards. Those standards require that we plan and perform the audit to obtain sufficient, appropriate evidence to provide a reasonable basis for our findings and conclusions based on our audit objectives. We believe that the evidence obtained provides a reasonable basis for our findings and conclusions based on our audit objectives

APPENDIX II: FERTILITY CONTROL AND GENETIC VARIABILITY

In addition to the information provided in this report to answer our primary objectives, we encountered two other issues related to BLM's management of the Wild Horse and Burro Program. The issues primarily relate to BLM's on-the-range management activities, including fertility control and genetic variability.

Fertility Control

BLM has been pursuing a fertility control vaccine called porcine zonae pellucida since 1992 to use as a tool for slowing the reproductive rate in wild horse populations. A slower reproductive rate would reduce the number of animals that would have to be gathered and removed, adopted, and held. BLM officials do not consider this treatment as the best short-term management tool to achieve AML but believe that once HMAs are at AML, fertility treatment can help to maintain that level. Much research has been conducted about the use of the vaccine in domestic and wild horses. The Department of the Interior's National Park Service has used this treatment to successfully manage wild horse populations at two national seashores. BLM field offices have been directed to consider the use of fertility control as an alternative in their gather plans, but they are not required to choose this research tool. The vaccine is considered experimental, and as such, there are barriers to its use. Since 2004, 47 HMAs have used fertility treatments, and a total of about 1,800 wild horses have been injected with the treatment. BLM considers the use of this treatment as a research tool; however, according to a prominent wild horse fertility researcher, BLM should more actively pursue its use as a management tool. According to BLM officials, fertility control may offer the possibility of reducing reproduction rates and costs, but BLM will still need to place horses in long-term holding in the future.

Genetic Variability

Herd health is another important component of BLM's on-the-range management of wild horses and burros. Specifically, it is important to maintain a degree of genetic variability to decrease the likelihood of disease and to maintain the biological fitness of the population. The amount of genetic variability that is sufficient to maintain a healthy population, however, is difficult to discern. Some groups have criticized BLM for setting AMLs at levels that are less than 100 or 150 animals. As of February 2008, 135 of the 199 HMAs had an upper limit of 150 or less for AML (see table 16). Several of these smaller HMAs, however, are part of a complex of HMAs that are managed as one unit where there is regular genetic interchange. For example, 13 complexes in Nevada encompass 45 of their 102 HMAs. According to a leading researcher in the field of wild horse genetics, however, a herd that has a population of less than 100 can be maintained with the introduction of at least one or two horses every 6 to 7 years, including those whose herd size are as small as 10 to 15 horses.

Table 16. Number of HMAs Managed at Various AMLs, February 2008

Upper limit of AML	Number of HMAs
0	8
1–100	102
101–150	25
151–200	16
201–300	25
301–500	16
501–1,000	5
Not yet determined	2
Total	**199**

Source: BLM.

BLM manages a few herds that show strong evidence of old Spanish heritage which no longer exists outside of the Americas. For example, the Kiger Mustangs of Oregon and the Pryor Mustangs of Montana have some colonial Spanish traits. For most of the HMAs, however, genetic variability is important primarily in maintaining the health of the herd, rather than managing for a specific genetic trait or bloodlines.

APPENDIX III: WILD HORSE AND BURRO SURVEY RESULTS

The following tables summarize responses collected through our survey instrument that was sent to 26 BLM field offices that manage HMAs. See appendix I for a complete explanation of which offices were chosen and the methodology used to select those field offices and specific HMAs. Our survey was divided into two sections. The first asked questions specific to the field offices' management of particular HMAs. The second section asked questions related to the field offices' general management of all HMAs.[2]

Section I: Field Office Responses Specific to Selected HMAs

Table 17. Current and Initial AML and Year of Determination per HMA Surveyed

HMA, by state	Initial AML	Year initial AML was set	Current AML	Year currentAML was set
Arizona				
Cibola–Trigo	315	1980	[a]	[a]
Lake Pleasant	80	1988	208	2000
Black Mountain	148	1978	478	1996
California				

[2] Eight of the 26 field offices surveyed manage only one HMA.

High Rock	70–100	1981	78–120	2001
Red Rock Lakes	16–25	1981	[a]	[a]
Centennial	168	1980	168	2005
Colorado				
Piceance–East Douglas Creek	90–140	1981	135–235	1999
Idaho				
Four Mile	37–60	2001	[a]	[a]
Montana				
Pryor Mountain Wild Horse Range	121	1984	95	1992
Nevada				
Montezuma Peak	161	1974	0	2007
South Shoshone	78	1986	60–100	2005
Flanigan	83–125	1990	[a]	[a]
Rock Creek	119	1987	250	2003
Dry Lake	82	1983	94	2001
Red Rock	116	1982	41–76	2004
Granite Range	155–258	1993	[a]	[a]
New Mexico				
Bordo Atravesado	20–30	1980	50	1991
Oregon				
Liggett Table	10–25	1989	[a]	[a]
Beaty's Butte	234	1971	100–250	1983
Coyote Lake–Alvord Tule Springs	198–390	1978	[a]	[a]
Utah				
Canyon Lands	60–100	2001	[a]	[a]
Hill Creek	195	1985	[a]	[a]
Conger	34	1977	40-80	1987
Wyoming				
Divide Basin	425–588	1979	415–600	1997
McCullough Peaks	70–140	1985	70–140	1990
Dishpan Butte	35–50	1983	50–100	1993

Source: GAO survey results.

[a] At the time of our survey, AML for 9 of the 26 HMAs we selected had not been revised since it was initially set. For those 9 HMAs, the initial AML and the year initial AML was set is also the current AML and the year current AML was set.

Table 18. Level of Data Sufficiency Used to Determine Current AML

Level of sufficiency	Number of respondents
Very sufficient	15
Moderately sufficient	7
Moderately insufficient	2
Very insufficient	1
Unsure/don't know	1

Source: GAO survey results.

Table 19. Respondents' Opinions about Current AML

Current AML	Number of respondents
Too high	3
About right	17
Too low	2
Unsure/don't know	4

Source: GAO survey results.

Table 20. Population Level in Comparison with AML Range

Population level	Number of respondents
Above	15
Within limits	10
Below	0
Unsure/don't know	1

Source: GAO survey results.

Table 21. Primary Challenges in Meeting or Maintaining AML

Challenge	Number of respondents
Impediments to conducting gathers	20
Lack of sufficient removal outlet	12
Inability to conduct range management	9
Limitations to accurate population counts	8
HMA boundary issues	5
Public pressure to not remove animals	4
Multiple use balance	4
Staffing limitations	3
Litigation	2
Habitat limitations	2
High reproductive rates of the animals	2
Other	2

Source: GAO survey results.

Table 22. Impact on Rangeland Resources in HMA When Herd Populations Exceed the Upper Limit of AML by Less Than 25 Percent

Rangeland resource	**Level of impact**					
	Positive	Slightly positive	No impact	Slightly negative	Negative	Blank
Horse and burro herd health	1	2	10	10	3	0
Rangeland health	0	1	5	10	10	0
Livestock habitat requirements	0	1	10	9	5	1
Wildlife habitat requirements	0	1	8	9	8	0

Source: GAO survey results.

Table 23. Impact on Rangeland Resources in HMA When Herd Populations Exceed the Upper Limit of AML by 25 to 50 Percent

Rangeland resource	**Level of impact**					
	Positive	Slightly positive	No impact	Slightly negative	Negative	Blank
Horse and burro herd health	1	1	4	10	10	0
Rangeland health	0	0	0	8	18	0
Livestock habitat requirements	0	0	4	9	12	1
Wildlife habitat requirements	0	0	3	8	15	0

Source: GAO survey results.

Table 24. Impact on Rangeland Resources in HMA When Herd Populations Exceed the Upper Limit of AML by 51 to 100 Percent

Rangeland resource	**Level of impact**					
	Positive	Slightly positive	No impact	Slightly negative	Negative	Blank
Horse and burro herd health	0	1	2	4	19	0
Rangeland health	0	0	0	0	26	0
Livestock habitat requirements	0	0	3	3	19	1
Wildlife habitat requirements	0	0	3	2	21	0

Source: GAO survey results.

Table 25. Number of Field Offices That Have or Do Not Have Procedures in Place to Distinguish Impact of Wild Horses and Burros, Cattle, and Wildlife on Rangeland Condition

Procedure to distinguish impact	Number of respondents
Yes	20
No	6
Unsure/don't know	0

Source: GAO survey results.

Table 26. Actions Taken to Manage HMAs Since 2000

Action taken	Yes	No	Don't know	Not applicable	Blank
Conducted population inventory	24	2	0	0	0
Conducted gathers and removals	23	3	0	0	0
Reduced or modified livestock use	15	7	0	4	0
Increased resource monitoring	14	10	2	0	0
Vegetative/riparian restoration	14	11	1	0	0
Other land management actions	12	2	1	2	9
Changed AML	**7**	**18**	**1**	**0**	**0**

Source: GAO survey results.

Table 27. Number of HMAs with a Herd Management Area Plan

Plan	Yes	No	Unsure/don't know
Herd Management Area Plan	16	9	1
Plan to develop a Herd Management Area Plan	8	2	5

Source: GAO survey results.

Table 28. Primary Physical Method Used in Most Recent Census/Inventory

Primary method	Number of respondents
Fixed-wing aircraft	3
Helicopter	20
Horseback/on foot	2
Don't know	1

Source: GAO survey results.

Table 29. Primary Statistical Method Used in Most Recent Census/Inventory

Primary method	Number of respondents
Direct count (single number)	17
Direct count (range)	2
Simultaneous double-count	3
Sightability bias correction model	2
Other	2

Source: GAO survey results.

Table 30. Level of Accuracy of Most Recent Census/Inventory

Level of accuracy	Number of respondents
Greatly over counted	0
Over counted	0
Counted about right	15
Undercounted	10
Greatly undercounted	0
Unsure/don't know	1

Source: GAO survey results.

Table 31. Level of Data Sufficiency Used to Support Most Recent Gather

Level of sufficiency	Number of respondents
Very sufficient	21
Moderately sufficient	4
Moderately insufficient	0
Very insufficient	0
Unsure/don't know	1

Source: GAO survey results.

Table 32. Timing of Gather in Relation to Scheduled Date of Gather

Timing of gather	Number of respondents
Conducted earlier	2
Neither earlier nor delayed	18
Delayed	4
Unsure/don't know	2

Source: GAO survey results.

Table 33. Level of AML to Which HMA Is Typically Gathered

Level of AML	Number of respondents
Upper	7
Middle	7
Lower	7
Unsure/don't know	5

Source: GAO survey results.

Section II: Field Offices' Responses to General Questions Regarding All of the HMAs they Manage

Table 34. Actions Taken to Manage HMA's Since 2000

Action taken	Yes	No	Don't know	Not applicable	Blank
Conducted population inventory	19	0	0	0	0
Conducted gathers and removals	18	1	0	0	0
Reduced or modified livestock use	14	2	1	2	0
Vegetative/riparian restoration	14	5	0	0	0
Increased resource monitoring	12	7	0	0	0
Changed AML	11	8	0	0	0
Other land management actions	6	2	1	0	10

Source: GAO survey results.

Table 35. Field Offices Whose HMAs Have Herd Management Area Plans

Plan	All	Some	None	Unsure/don't know
Herd Management Area Plan	11	6	8	1

Source: GAO survey results.

Table 36. Field Offices Working to Develop Herd Management Area Plans for All of Their HMAs

Response	Number of respondents
Yes	6
No	8

Source: GAO survey results.

Table 37. Actions to Help Field Offices Achieve Healthy Herd Populations in Balance with the Range and Other Multiple Uses

Actions	Number of respondents
Increase range management activities	15
Reach and maintain AML	9
Improve staff capacity	7
Improve census/inventory	7
Increase funding	6
Improve adoption outlet	3
Improve coordination in management	3
Improve access to HMAs	2
Solve long-term holding situation	2

Source: GAO survey results.

Table 38. Major Challenges Facing Field Offices in Managing HMAs to Achieve Healthy Herd Populations that Are in Balance with the Range and other Multiple Uses

Major challenges	Number of respondents
Impediments to conducting gathers	13
Staffing limitations	11
Limitations to accurate population counts	8
Inability to conduct range management	8
Multiple use balance	7
Lack of sufficient removal outlet	6
Ability to maintain AML	4
Habitat limitations	4
Other 4	
Planning process	3
Public pressure	3
HMA boundary issues	3

Source: GAO survey results.

Table 39. Major Challenges Facing BLM's Wild Horse and Burro Program As a Whole

Major challenges	Number of respondents
Lack of sufficient removal outlet[a]	18
Staffing limitations	11
Inability to conduct range management	8
Public pressure	7
Impediments to conducting gathers	5
Unwanted horses released to BLM lands	5
Funding	3
Lack of support	3
Limitations to accurate population counts	2
Habitat limitations	2
Lack of management flexibility	2
Multiple use balance	2
Poor public perception	2

Source: GAO survey results.

[a] Removal outlet limitations include decreased options for animals once removed from the range, such as decreased adoptions, expense of caring for animals removed from the range, and limited capacity in long-term holding facilities.

APPENDIX IV: COMMENTS FROM THE DEPARTMENT OF THE INTERIOR

United States Department of the Interior
BUREAU OF LAND MANAGEMENT
Washington, DC 20240
http://www.blm.gov

TAKE PRIDE IN AMERICA

SEP 0 5 2008

Robin M. Nazzaro
Director, Natural Resources and Environment
Government Accountability Office
441 G Street, N.W.
Washington, D.C. 20548-0001

Dear Ms. Nazzaro:

Thank you for the opportunity to review and comment on the Government Accountability Office draft report entitled, *"Bureau of Land Management: Effective Long-Term Options Needed to Manage Unadoptable Wild Horses,* (GAO-08-989).

The Department of the Interior concurs with the findings and recommendations for executive action and believes these will help us improve the Wild Horses and Burro Program. The Bureau of Land Management will work to develop cost effective alternatives to long term holding. BLM will seek advice from the National Wild Horse and Burro Advisory Board and other partners and stakeholders to find acceptable solutions, and will discuss any helpful legislative proposals with Congress.

The enclosure provides technical comments on the draft report.

If you have any questions, please contact Don Glenn, Chief, Division of Wild Horses and Burros at (202) 452-5082 or LaVanna Stevenson-Harris, BLM Audit Liaison Officer, at (202) 785-6580.

Sincerely,

James L. Caswell
Director

Enclosure

ENDNOTES

[1] Pub. L. No. 92-195, 85 Stat. 649 (1971) (codified as amended at 16 U.S.C. §§ 1331–1340).

[2] This report focuses solely on BLM's Wild Horse and Burro Program. BLM is responsible for managing over 90 percent of the wild horses and burros on public lands. The Forest Service is responsible for managing 2,200 wild horses and about 300 burros in 37 Wild Horse Territories that cover about 2.5 million acres of Forest Service land.

[3] Shortly after the 1971 act, BLM conducted a wild horse and burro population census and estimated the number of wild horses to be about 17,300 and the number of wild burros to be about 8,000.

[4] The 44 BLM field units include 39 field offices, 4 district offices in Oregon, and 1 field station—the Tonopah Field Station in Nevada. We will refer to these 44 BLM field units collectively as field offices. BLM's count of the number of offices that manage HMAs may differ because the 4 district offices in Oregon manage 7 resource area offices.

[5] Pub. L. No. 95-514, § 14, 92 Stat. 1803, 1808 (1978) (amending 16 U.S.C. §§ 1332–1333).

[6] *Animal Protection Institute of America*, 109 IBLA 112, 119 (1989) (internal quotes omitted).

[7] This total does not include the number of burros removed from the range in 1981. BLM was not able to verify older data or estimate the number of burro removals for 1981. The total number of wild horses and burros that BLM could verify were removed from the range between 1971 and 2007 was 249,489. Officials verified that the number of animals removed between 1977 and 1980 was 18,009; however, they were unable to further specify this number by year or by species. When added together, this total equals 267,498.

[8] 16 U.S.C. § 1333(b)(2)(B).

[9] 16 U.S.C. § 1333(b)(2)(C) (destroy excess animals for which an adoption demand does not exist) and 16 U.S.C. § 1333(e) (sell without limitation excess animals under certain circumstances).

[10] Pub. L. No. 108-447, Div. E, Title I, § 142, 118 Stat. 2809, 3070 (2004) (amending 16 U.S.C. § 1333). In 2005, shortly after the 2004 sales directive was enacted, legislation was introduced in the 109th Congress that would have prohibited the sale of wild horses and burros for processing into commercial products (H.R. 297 and S. 576). Neither of these bills were enacted. More recently, in the 110th Congress, H.R. 249 was introduced to prohibit the sale of wild horses and burros for processing into commercial products. The bill was passed by the House of Representatives on April 26, 2007. As of August 31, 2008, the Senate had not acted on the bill.

[11] The number 567,000 represents the cattle yearlong equivalent derived by dividing the actual number of animal unit months billed in fiscal year 2007 by 12 months. An animal unit month refers to the amount of forage needed to sustain an adult cow and her calf or horse for 1 month. In reality, few livestock grazing permits are issued for yearlong grazing.

[12] BLM manages wild horses and burros on 199 HMAs that are comprised of 29 million acres of BLM land and an additional 5.35 million acres of non-BLM land.

[13] GAO, *Rangeland Management: Improvements Needed in Federal Wild Horse Program*, GAO/RCED-90-110 (Washington, D.C.: Aug. 20, 1990).

[14] We drew our sample of 26 field units from among the 44 field units that manage HMAs, which include 39 field offices, 4 district offices in Oregon, and 1 field station in Nevada. BLM's count of the number of offices that manage HMAs may differ because the 4 district offices in Oregon manage 7 resource area offices.

[15] Pub. L. No. 92-196, § 9, 85 Stat. 649, 651 (renumbered as § 10 of the act and codified at 16 U.S.C. § 1339).

[16] Pub. L. No. 92-196, § 4, 85 Stat. 649, 651 (codified at 16 U.S.C. § 1334).

[17] Three of the 199 HMAs are classified as Wild Horse Ranges—the Pryor Mountains Wild Horse Range in Montana, the Little Book Cliffs Wild Horse Range in Colorado, and the

Nevada Wild Horse Range of south-central Nevada. One of the HMAs is classified as a Wild Burro Range—the Marietta Wild Burro Range located in Nevada. According to the 1971 act, under certain circumstances, the Secretaries of the Interior and Agriculture may designate and maintain specific ranges on public lands as sanctuaries for the protection and preservation of wild free-roaming horses and burros. 16 U.S.C. § 1333(a). Ranges are to be devoted principally, but not necessarily exclusively, to their welfare in keeping with the multiple-use management concept for the public lands. 16 U.S.C. § 1332(c). BLM can also choose to close appropriate areas of public lands to grazing use by all or a particular kind of livestock, if necessary, to provide habitat for wild horses or burros; to implement herd management actions; or to protect wild horses or burros from disease, harassment, or injury. 43 C.F.R. § 4710.5.

[18] *Animal Protection Institute of America*, 109 IBLA at 119 (internal quotes omitted).

[19] Some HMAs report AML as a single number rather than as a range; however, they also calculate an upper and lower limit of AML to determine the level within which to manage herds. BLM is drafting guidance to direct all field offices to identify AML as a range.

[20] According to BLM officials, as of February 2008, the upper limit of AML nationally was approximately 27,219 animals, and the lower limit of AML was approximately 17,957. Based on our calculation, the midpoint between the two limits is approximately 22,588. These numbers are considered approximate because not all HMAs report AML as a range. AML for 7 HMAs are reported as the midpoint of AML, while 29 HMAs report AML as the upper limit. Therefore, to account for the 36 HMAs that report a single AML number, BLM may only approximate the true upper, lower, and midpoint of AML on a nationwide basis.

[21] BLM has gather contracts with two private companies.

[22] The selective removal policy is used only for wild horses; it is not applicable to wild burros. When gathers are conducted, an emphasis is placed on removing the younger, more adoptable animals from the range. However, the sex ratio and age structure of the herd must also be considered to assure a healthy population

[23] U.S. Department of the Interior, BLM, *Living Legends in Balance with the Land, A Strategy to Achieve Healthy Lands and Viable Herds, The Restoration of Threatened Watersheds Initiative* (Washington, D.C., 2000).

[24] The number of HMAs managed by BLM has changed over time. In 2002, BLM managed 208 HMAs, 142 of which had set AML, or 68 percent.

[25] *Dahl v. Clark*, 600 F. Supp. 585 (Dist. Ct. Nev. 1984).

[26] For this report we reviewed BLM's process for making AML determinations and the factors it considers during that process. We are not expressing a legal opinion as to whether any individual AML established through this process would achieve and maintain a "thriving natural ecological balance," as required by the act. 16 U.S.C. § 1333(a), (b)(2); *see also, Animal Protection Institute of America*, 109 IBLA 112, 115.

[27] Under Section 7 of the Endangered Species Act, all federal agencies must ensure that any actions they authorize, fund, or carry out are not likely to jeopardize the continued existence of a listed species or result in the destruction or adverse modification of its designated critical habitat.

[28] GAO/RCED-90-110.

[29] An animal unit month refers to the amount of forage needed to sustain an adult cow and her calf or horse for 1 month.

[30] U.S. Department of the Interior, BLM, Gather Policy and Selective Removal Criteria, Instruction Memorandum No. 2005-206 (Washington, D.C., Aug. 10, 2005). Although the instruction memorandum had an expiration date of September 30, 2006, according to BLM officials, it is still considered to be in effect until it is reissued.

[31] According to BLM, the effort to revise the *Wild Horse and Burro Program Handbook* was first initiated in 1997. The effort was restarted most recently in 2006 when the draft handbook was significantly rewritten and expanded.

[32] S. Rpt. 99-141, at 6, 121 (1985).

[33] Rangeland health standards were developed to be consistent with the fundamentals of rangeland health, including watersheds that are in a properly functioning condition; ecological processes that are maintained in order to support healthy biotic populations and communities; water quality that complies with state water quality standards; and habitats that are being restored or maintained for federal threatened and endangered species, proposed or candidate threatened and endangered species, and other special status species.

[34] GAO/RCED-90-110.

[35] U.S. Department of the Interior, BLM, Gather Policy and Selective Removal Criteria, Instruction Memorandum No. 2005-206 (Washington, D.C., Aug. 10, 2005). The 2005 policy updated BLM Instruction Memorandum No. 2002-095, dated February13, 2002. The 2002 policy did not explicitly enumerate the key factors that should be considered as part of the gather and removal analysis.

[36] U.S. Department of the Interior, BLM, Establishment/Adjustment of Appropriate Management Levels, and Managing Planned Escalating Problem and Emergency Gathers, Instruction Memorandum No. 2004-151 (Washington, D.C., Mar. 16, 2004). When gathers are conducted as a result of an emergency, such as a fire, a National Environmental Policy Act analysis and gather plans are still required prior to the animal removal, if time permits. If immediate action is required, emergency actions should be documented and a report prepared after resolution of the problem.

[37] The five methods experts are investigating include the following: (1) Photographic mark-resight involves two or more separate counts. First, an aerial count is conducted, and each group of animals photographed. This is followed soon after by additional aerial counts. The photographs from each survey are compared to determine which animals were seen on each pass and which were missed. A statistical technique to estimate the number missed is based on the number missing on each pass. (2) Simultaneous double-count is a form of mark-resight that uses only one count where two observers in an aircraft independently observe and record a direct count of wild horses or burros. Sighting rates are estimated by comparing sighting records of the two observers, and the number of horses that were missed by both individuals can be estimated. (3) Sightability bias correction involves observers that count animals but also records other factors about each sighting, such as if the groups were large or small, terrain type, weather, and other factors that may have prevented some animals from being seen. (4) Distance sampling estimates the number of animals or herds based on the distance and location of the animals that are seen on the ground. The data enables statisticians to predict the number of animals that are not seen because they are too far away. (5) Combined techniques utilize different

combinations of the aforementioned four techniques to mitigate known biases associated with each individual method.

[38] Demand for burros has stayed relatively stable from an annual average of 1,154 burros adopted from 1990 through 1999 and an annual average of 1,092 burros adopted from 2000 through 2007.

[39] The last horse slaughterhouse in the United States closed in fall 2007. The number of domestic horses killed in slaughterhouses from 2000 to 2005 ranged from about 40,000 to 75,000 annually. Without these outlets, more domestic horses are available to the public, causing direct competition with wild horse adoptions and sales.

[40] Three of these facilities were added to incorporate horse gentling programs to improve the likelihood of adoption.

[41] Long-term holding costs were, on average, $1.20 in 2000, $1.22 in 2001, and $1.25 per horse per day from 2001 through 2004. In 2005, the cost increased to $1.27 per horse per day through 2007 and will increase to $1.28 per horse per day by the end of 2008.

[42] GAO/RCED-90-110.

[43] U.S. Department of the Interior, Office of Inspector General, Selected Aspects of the Wild Horse and Burro Program (Washington, D.C., May 1994).

[44] Standards for internal control in the federal government describe internal controls as "a series of actions and activities that occur throughout an [agency's] operations and on an ongoing basis" used "to regulate and guide [the agency's] operations." See GAO, Standards for Internal Control in the Federal Government, GAO/AIMD-00-21.3.1 (Washington, D.C.: November 1999).

[45] For 2007, BLM also reported 616 births in short-term holding facilities.

[46] For 2007, BLM also reported 303 births in long-term holding facilities. Although studs are gelded prior to being sent to long-term holding and the wild horses are separated by sex, pregnant mares may be transferred from short-term holding facilities into long-term holding facilities.

[47] *Empacadora de Carnes de Fresnillo v. Curry*, 476 F.3d 326 (5th Cir. 2007), cert. denied, 75 U.S.L.W. 3569 (U.S. May 21, 2007). *See also,* Tex. Agric. Code Ann. §§ 149.001-149.007.

[48] *Cavel Int'l, Inc. v. Madigan*, 500 F.3d 551 (7th Cir. 2007), cert. denied, 76 U.S.L.W. 3410 (U.S. June 16, 2008). *See also,* 225 Ill. Comp. Stat. 635/1.5.

[49] Current legislation pending in the 110th Congress (H.R. 503 and S. 311) would prohibit the commercial sale of horses to foreign countries, such as Canada and Mexico, to be slaughtered for human consumption.

[50] 16 U.S.C. § 1333(b)(2)(C).

[51] GAO/RCED-90-110.

[52] 16 U.S.C. § 1333(e)(1).

[53] 16 U.S.C. § 1333(e)(2).

[54] H.R. 249, 110th Cong. (2007). The bill was passed by the House of Representatives on April 26, 2007. As of August 31, 2008, the Senate had not acted on the bill.

INDEX

A

B

D

E

F

J

K

L

M

N

O

P

Q

R

S

T

U

V

W

Y